VICTOR AND
VICTIM

THIS VOLUME INCORPORATES THE SUBSTANCE
OF FOUR LECTURES DELIVERED ON THE
SIR D. OWEN EVANS FOUNDATION AT THE
UNIVERSITY COLLEGE OF WALES, ABERYSTWYTH
DURING THE SESSION 1958

VICTOR AND VICTIM

THE CHRISTIAN DOCTRINE
OF REDEMPTION

BY

J. S. WHALE

CAMBRIDGE
AT THE UNIVERSITY PRESS
1960

PUBLISHED BY

THE SYNDICS OF THE CAMBRIDGE UNIVERSITY PRESS

Bentley House, 200 Euston Road, London, N.W. 1
American Branch: 32 East 57th Street, New York 22, N.Y.

©

CAMBRIDGE UNIVERSITY PRESS

1960

TO
DAVID

CONTENTS

PREFACE   *page* vii

I   THE FULNESS OF TIME   1

II   CHRIST'S VICTORY OVER SATAN   20

III CHRIST OUR SACRIFICIAL VICTIM   42

IV   THE CROSS AS JUDGMENT AND PENALTY   61

V   THE OFFENCE OF PARTICULARITY   80

VI   THE REDEEMED SOCIETY   98

VII BAPTISM AND EUCHARIST   118

VIII THE BODY OF CHRIST AND RESURRECTION   148

     INDEX   168

PREFACE

The sole justification for a preface to the chapters which follow is an expression of my indebtedness and thanks.

I am grateful to Miss Kathleen Raine for readily allowing me to quote from an article on the work of the late Edwin Muir.

I am also indebted to the courtesy of publishers who have given me permission to make quotations from certain books, details of which are given in the footnotes. In particular, my grateful acknowledgments are due to the Syndics of the Cambridge University Press (F. M. Cornford, *The Unwritten Philosophy and other Essays*; C. H. Dodd, *The Bible To-day*); to the Delegates of the Oxford University Press (R. G. Collingwood, *The Idea of History*; R. Otto, *The Idea of the Holy*); to the Chicago University Press (P. Tillich, *Systematic Theology*); to Thomas Nelson and Sons Ltd. (The Revised Standard Version of the Bible); to the Student Christian Movement Press (K. Barth, *The Teaching of the Church regarding Baptism*; J. A. T. Robinson, *The Body*; P. Tillich, *The New Being*); to James Nisbet and Co. Ltd. (P. Tillich, *The Courage to Be*); to Longmans, Green and Co. Ltd. (G. W. H. Lampe, *Reconciliation in Christ*); to Ernest Benn Ltd. (W. J. Turner, *Beethoven: The Search for Reality*); and to Hodder and Stoughton Ltd. (C. F. D. Moule, *The Sacrifice of Christ*). The two poems by Alice Meynell are reproduced by kind permission and by arrangement with Burns, Oates and Washbourne, Ltd.

PRINCETON UNIVERSITY   J. S. W.
1 February 1960

CHAPTER I

THE FULNESS OF TIME

We assume that time is real, and no illusion. This is the obvious meaning of our clocks and calendars, our diaries and anniversaries. But what is time? We cannot say. Our attempts at definition break down because they always include some temporal reference, and so beg the question: they make use of the very thing to be defined, which is like explaining a liquid as something wet, or describing a flame in terms of combustion. In the *Physics* Aristotle defined time as the measure of motion, only to add that motion is also the measure of time.[1] In short, a mystery which is resolved in terms óf itself must remain a mystery. It was the profound and subtle mind of St Augustine which gave classic expression to this difficulty when he wrote: 'If anyone asks me what time is I cannot say; if no one asks me I know very well.'[2]

The Christian gospel of redemption is rooted in history. It is no inference from *a priori* arguments for the being and nature of God, but the dynamic self-disclosure of the living God himself in certain events of historic time. The central declaration of Christianity is not that God is something but that he has done something. 'When the time had fully come God sent forth his Son, born of woman, born under the law, to redeem those who were under the law.' What does this mean for the Christian understanding of time?

The name of Karl Barth reminds us that much modern theology insists on being strictly and exclusively biblical. It repudiates the concern of scholastic theology with philosophy and asks, as

[1] οὐ μόνον δὲ τὴν κίνησιν τῷ χρόνῳ μετροῦμεν, ἀλλὰ καὶ τῇ κινήσει τὸν χρόνον διὰ τὸ ὁρίζεσθαι ὑπ' ἀλλήλων (*Phys.* IV, xii, 220 b 15).

[2] Nulla tempora tibi coaeterna sunt quia tu permanes; et illa, si permanerent, non essent tempora. . . . Quid est ergo tempus? Si nemo ex me quaeret, scio; si quaerenti explicare velim, nescio (*Conf.* xi. 14).

Tertullian did, what Jerusalem has to do with Athens. But, cogent though this is, we should not allow ourselves to be browbeaten by it. If an Aquinas could look back profitably to Aristotle, and an Anselm to Plato, we may be allowed to approach the great problem of eternity and time, not by the obviously direct way of our Hebraic-Christian heritage, but indirectly by way of that other heritage which is also ours, the Hellenism of the ancient world into which Christianity came. There is much to be learned from standing, first, with the Greeks in the Court of the Gentiles.

I

If I may affix a fashionable label to it, Greek thought was existential. It was dominated by a sense of contrast between existence and essence; between the flux and change of things which are ever coming to be or ceasing to be and the constant, unchanging order of eternal reality. The central Greek tradition subordinated the temporal to the timeless, process to reality. It was an eager and obstinate search for the ἀκίνητον, that unmoved and changeless reality, knowledge of which was the only real knowledge.

Its first triumph was geometry. Empirically speaking, no straight line which we can draw is perfectly straight and without breadth; and no flat surface, however smoothly polished, is perfectly plane. Each is no more than an approximation when seen under a microscope. But straight line or plane as the mathematician thinks of them involve no physical objects at all. As eternal entities they transcend representation by pencil and paper. Microscopic scrutiny is irrelevant. Because a right-angled triangle is timelessly what it is, the theorem of Pythagoras is real knowledge.

The next step was Plato's. Though no individual thing gives us a perfect example of its characteristic qualities, it is nevertheless what it is because it participates in its essential 'idea'. Though no particular circle is perfect it participates in the eternal idea of circularity. Each beautiful thing is beautiful because it participates in the eternal form or idea of beauty which it imperfectly resembles.

Plato's system is built on this doctrine. All that belongs to each science may be grouped as a series of ideas graded hierarchically under a leading Idea. Further, the respective ideas of all the sciences, moral as well as physical, form a systematic unity, a great unified structure at the head of which stands the idea of the Good. All the ideas are subordinate or departmental expressions of this crowning Idea. The idea of circularity, for example, is an expression of mathematical good. The idea of justice is an expression of good in human relationship. The idea of beauty is the expression of good in things visible or audible, such as sculpture or music. Thus the ultimate explanation of any particular thing lies in some expression of the good which it attempts, but fails, to realize.

Platonism points steadily to this failure. Like all the great forms of existentialism it separates existence from essence, the transitory world of sense from the world of pure, unchanging ideas. The ideas exist apart, in the heavenly places; and the particularities of the temporal order are, at best, pale reflections or copies (μιμήματα) of the good which is 'laid up in heaven'. Plato refuses to concede the full reality of the temporal process. Only the αἰώνιος is ἀληθινός. Eternal being alone is real.

This being so, the supremely important question asked by Plato's age concerned the nature and destiny of man. The answer came from Orphic and Pythagorean religion and, as befitting a religion of redemption, it corresponded to a threefold norm.

Orphism declared, first, that the human soul had pre-existed from eternity as a spiritual, immortal substance, participating directly in essential being. Man, therefore, is 'a heavenly, not an earthly plant' (φυτὸν οὐκ ἔγγειον ἀλλ' οὐράνιον).[1]

Its second declaration was that man's existence contradicts what he essentially is; he is, in some sense, a fallen being; his true essentiality has been lost. It is not a complete loss, however, for he 'remembers' it. In the temporal, material order of nature to which the human body belongs, the soul is an unwilling prisoner. Indeed, as Plato put it, the body is a tomb;[2] and, when true to itself, the soul seeks release and separation from bodily existence.

[1] τὸ μὲν σῶμά ἐστιν ἡμῖν σῆμα (*Gorgias*, 493 A). Cf. *Cratylus*, 400 C.
[2] Plato, *Timaeus*, 90 A.

Its third declaration, therefore, was that salvation means the soul's escape and return to its true home in the eternal order: either through purifying rites, as in Orphism, or by contemplative participation in the true and the good, as in Platonist philosophy proper.

This brief survey of its fundamental presuppositions will indicate why Greek thought was little interested in history. The events of time exemplify that world of ceaseless change which the Greek genius sought to transcend. Aristotle's dictum that philosophy is more important than history, and poetry more beautiful, is typically Greek. It anticipates and explains the kindred Stoic dictum that the wise man is not concerned with time.

At first glance it seems strange that this type of thought – clearly incompatible with the Hebraic-Christian gospel which overthrew it – should have had a strong and almost unbroken influence on Christianity through the centuries.

The incompatibility is indisputable, as two fundamental affirmations of the Christian creed suffice to show. First, the Christian doctrine of creation denies that there is anything eternal save God: all that is not God was created by him 'out of nothing'. This leaves no room either for a transcendent order of eternal forms existing from eternity, or for the human soul as uncreated and immortal. Second, the Christian gospel of incarnation and redemption witnesses to a dynamic self-disclosure of the eternal within the temporal: the Creator himself is the Redeemer: the eternal Word becomes flesh in historic time: the Impassible suffers:[1] the Immortal dies. This is 'to the Greeks foolishness',[2] and it is plainly incompatible with the Platonist-Gnostic conception of pure Being, transcendent, impersonal and changeless, all untroubled by the temporal process of Becoming, which is pervaded by suffering, sin and death. Could incompatibility be more complete? And must not the sons of Zion therefore confront the sons of Greece like a brandished sword?[3]

[1] ἀπαθῶς ἔπαθεν, found in Gregory of Nyssa, is a typical patristic paradox.
[2] I Cor. i. 23.
[3] Zech. ix. 13.

4

But though this dichotomy between Hebraism and Hellenism, popularized by Matthew Arnold, is familiar and accepted, it becomes increasingly dubious to modern research, especially since the discovery of the Dead Sea Scrolls. And even if this were not so, is the admitted incompatibility as clear and complete as contrasted *credenda* might suggest? The question is unavoidable because the Christian centuries witness to a kinship between Hebraism and Hellenism in spite of their manifest incompatibility. Can it be denied that Platonism has something in common with the essential meaning of the Christian doctrines of creation and providence? By refusing to concede that the temporal process is fully real Plato does not say that it is quite unrelated to eternal Being. There *is* a relation, though Socrates does not know how it is to be described (a modest agnosticism from which confident dogmatists in later ages could have learned with profit). The eternal is somehow active in the temporal, sustaining it in all its parts. Again, the Platonist and Christian evaluations of man's situation coincide rather than conflict in that each uses the symbolism of a fall from essential perfection. Again, St Paul can say that the things which are seen are temporal but the things which are unseen are eternal: one of many indications within the New Testament that Christianity and Platonism are akin in their common awareness that this world of time and sense cannot ultimately suffice us, made as we are in God's image. 'Here we have no continuing city, but we seek one to come.'[1] Wordsworth's great Ode describes our mother earth as the homely nurse, doing all she can

> To make her foster-child, her inmate Man
>   Forget the glories he hath known,
> And that imperial palace whence he came.

This is Platonism. But it is not radically different from the transcendentalism of the Christian hymn,

> I'm but a stranger here,
> Heaven is my home.

For Hebraism as well as for Hellenism the true evaluation of this

[1] Heb. xiii. 14.

world has to be made against the background of its impermanence.

This is a long way, admittedly, from John iii. 16. We are as yet only in the outer court of the Temple. But it is not as bad a place to be in as ardent protagonists of strictly biblical theology contend. Indeed, one of the plainest facts of Christian history is that, rightly or wrongly, Christian theology has been prone to linger here.

The evidence for this is not absent from the New Testament even though the research of the past fifty years has shown its thought and language to be predominantly Semitic rather than Greek. The same evidence is writ large in the Christian Platonists of Alexandria; in the neo-Platonism which passed into the blood-stream of the Church as Catholic mysticism; in that most complex of all the giant figures in the long history of Christian doctrine, the Platonist-Biblicist Augustine; in Franciscan scholasticism; in the Renaissance Platonism of the Florentine academy; in John Colet; in the Cambridge Platonists; and – to cut short a list which, if full, would be quite unmanageable – in modern platonizing theologians as diverse as Dean Inge and Paul Elmer More, A. E. Taylor and Paul Tillich. This continuous ecclesiastical tradition gives support to Whitehead's dictum that European thought itself is 'a series of footnotes to Plato'.

These footnotes vary in their respective details, but their uniform relevance to the issue before us lies in their common reluctance to allow that time is man's ultimate concern. Time is, at best, a second best; it is but the moving image of eternity; a copy or shadow – no more – of the timeless perfection of pure universality.

> Was sich nie und nirgends hat begeben,
> Das allein veraltet nie.[1]

And this virtual indifference to history in a Spinoza, or a Schopenhauer, becomes something like hostility in a Bosanquet. According to Collingwood, Bosanquet treated history with open contempt as a false form of thought.[2]

---

[1] That which ne'er and nowhere has befallen,
That alone it is which cannot age.

[2] *The Idea of History* (Oxford, 1956), p. 143.

This brings us to the crucial issue: *How important is history?* It is an issue to which three main answers are given.

The first answer is that history does not ultimately matter. In the tradition at which we have been looking – the Aryan tradition of Hellenism, to which we may add that of philosophical Hinduism – history makes no difference to eternity, nor does eternity make any difference to it. It is no more than a momentary ripple on the infinite ocean of Being. The vertical dimension, expressed in soaring spire or fountain, symbolizes the eternal which is alone real. The hold of such transcendentalism on the Eastern as well as on the Western mind has weakened notoriously in recent decades, but it is still powerful: John MacMurray has even called it the most serious disease of contemporary spirituality.

The second answer is the polar opposite of this. It is given by the various forms of naturalism. To revert to the dimensional metaphor, it substitutes the horizontal for the vertical. It insists stoutly on the ultimacy of the seen and temporal. 'Your wistful yearning for the transcendent and eternal', it says, 'is irrelevant if not meaningless. Forget it. All the varied richness elaborated by the temporal process will come at length to the darkness and nothingness of death: this is the common and inevitable end for individuals, societies, civilizations and the great globe itself. Accept it. Facts are facts; all else is fantasy.' This attitude, too, is still powerful, if not dominant in the contemporary world. We may call it the most serious disease of contemporary secularity.

The third answer is given by the Hebraic-Christian tradition. It affirms the polar relatedness of what is true in each of these opposed attitudes. Its distinctive genius is as much this-worldly as other-worldly. Its central declaration is not only that God is what he is, the eternal heaven of pure Being; but also that he is *deus actuosus*, the Creator of the world and its Recreator; he has entered into the valley of the shadow to redeem it. In the actuality of certain historic events the ontologically remote is also dynamically near, 'mighty to save'. The eternal is in active, personal, moral and redemptive relation with the temporal. To know this; to know that the eternal is the living God and the lord of history, is to have left the outer Court of the Gentiles and to have entered the Temple.

II

Here the Hebrew prophets are speaking. Israel's understanding of redemption is dominated by the insight of men who are neither philosophers nor mystics, properly speaking. They do not conceive of redemption in Platonist, Orphic or Gnostic fashion as the liberation of the spiritual part of a man at the moment of death from an unredeemable world of time and corruption to which his body belongs. For them redemption is a process at work in history; the history of Israel.

Orphism was concerned with biography rather than history. It interpreted redemption as a spiritual ἄσκησις or discipline whereby each individual might prepare for his escape from 'this muddy vesture of decay' at death. The prophets are concerned with the corporate history of Israel, notably at the Exodus and at Sinai: that is, with the redeeming activity of the living God in the stuff of events, whereby he may make for himself a people. For an Amos or an Isaiah, therefore, time is no shadow or copy of the eternal but the actual context and condition of the eternal God's speech to Israel and of Israel's response thereto. Time is sacramental in the sense that it is the vehicle of the eternal God's activity; the means whereby he discloses himself as holy and expresses his will as law; the roaring loom on which his mighty acts of judgment and mercy are woven. Because time is the form through which will necessarily expresses itself, Israel's history (and ultimately all history)[1] gives actuality to the purpose of God.

The prophets understand time, then, in terms of will: the purposive will of God and the responsive will of man. Certain events in Israel's history make continuously actual a relationship between God and man so close and intimate that it is constantly understood and described as a covenant relationship.[2] This is no contract of mutual convenience terminable at will by either side;

[1] See p. 93, below.
[2] See p. 48, below.

8

it is as inherently indissoluble as is the relationship between a son and his father. To the philosophical Greek mind such a relationship between the infinite and the finite is unintelligible and foolish: to Israel it is the supreme issue, the final meaning and the ultimate glory of human existence. History matters. Here in the Temple the wise man, God's servant the prophet, is concerned with time. Time is the vehicle not only of divine revelation but of human response. Time is God's time and he is sovereign lord of it. Thus the concern which pervades the prophetic understanding of history is a moral concern. Knowing the truth means doing the truth. The inescapable content of time (empty time being inconceivable) is decision and action. This means that man may do but two things with time: he may misuse it, or use it to God's glory, 'redeeming the time', making the most of every opportunity which it presents. What he cannot do is to live in a neutral dimension of timelessness where there would be no acts of will, and therefore no effective vindication of the divine purpose.

Throughout the Christian centuries great moralists, our latter-day prophets, have been prone to linger here in the Temple, witnessing to 'categorical imperative' and to duty as 'stern daughter of the voice of God'. Puritanism, both in its Catholic and its Protestant forms, is an expression of this moral urgency in the Hebraic understanding of time. Richard Baxter's lament that he had 'been sensible, these forty years, of the sin of wasted time' links him with St Benedict and St Jerome as well as with Mill and Carlyle, John Morley and Martineau. The very Victorians who rebelled against Christian orthodoxy owed their high sense of life as a 'swift and solemn trust' to Israel's prophetic awareness that time is no clockwork sequence of neutral moments, but the ordinance of God himself for the fulfilment of his purpose in creation.

But here we meet a notorious difficulty. Who can meet this unconditional divine demand of which time is the symbol? The sublime moralism which braces man for heights of victorious achievement also mirrors his sin and failure, and reduces him to

9

despair. The too much quoted question of the prophet Micah, 'What doth the Lord require of thee but to do justly, and to love mercy, and to walk humbly with thy God?', is not sentimental idealism but devastating judgment. Man is not only judged and doomed, he is also mocked, if this threefold divine imperative is God's only way of dealing with him. Empirically considered he cannot redeem the time, making the most of every opportunity for justice, mercy and humility which offers. 'Not the labours of my hands can fulfil thy laws demands.' It is the dilemma of all ethical religion that the higher the conception of God's holiness the more impassable is the gulf between man and his only source of salvation. Unless there is in the Temple a gospel of God's grace in forgiveness, vindicating yet transcending the judgment of his holy law, who can escape final condemnation? 'I wept much,' records the seer of the Apocalypse, 'because no man was able.'[1]

Does God add nothing, then, to the word of judgment and doom uttered through his servants the prophets? Is there no pattern of forgiveness and renewal in their understanding of Israel's history and of universal history, anticipating that gospel which evoked Luther's ecstatic cry of gratitude '*Er hat noch ein Wort*' (He has another word)? To this question St Augustine gave the succinct and classic answer that in the Old Testament the New is latent, and in the New Testament the Old is patent. Here the great doctor of grace, writing as biblical theologian rather than as Christian Platonist, was vindicating the unity of the scriptures and their evangelical genius. For essential to the prophetic interpretation of history is what has been called its 'two-beat rhythm': that is, the holiness of God visiting her iniquities upon Israel in judgment and disaster, *and yet* renewing her life in mercy and redemption. As the distinguished Calvinist theologian Auguste Lecerf once observed to me, 'the key to the Old Testament is the word *nevertheless*'. He was thinking, presumably, of the two-beat rhythm of justice and mercy, law and grace, to which passages such as these bear witness:

[1] Rev. v. 3 – 4.

I said in my heart, I am cut off from before thine eyes: *nevertheless* thou heardest the voice of my supplications when I cried unto thee. (Ps. xxxi. 22.)

Thou broughtest us into the net; thou laid'st affliction upon our loins. Thou hast caused men to ride over our heads; we went through fire and water: *but* thou broughtest us out into a wealthy place. (Ps. lxvi. 11 – 12.)

So foolish was I and ignorant: I was as a beast before thee. *Nevertheless* I am continually with thee; thou hast holden me by my right hand. (Ps. lxxiii. 22 – 3.)

Then will I visit their transgression with the rod, and their iniquity with stripes. *Nevertheless*, my loving kindness will I not utterly take from him.
(Ps. lxxxix. 32 – 3.)

Our fathers understood not thy wonders in Egypt; they remembered not the multitude of thy mercies; but provoked him at the sea, even at the Red Sea. *Nevertheless*, he saved them for his name's sake. (Ps. cvi. 7 – 8.)

Many times did he deliver them; but they provoked him with their counsel, and were brought low for their iniquity. *Nevertheless* he regarded their affliction when he heard their cry. (Ps. cvi. 43 – 4.)

For thus saith the Lord God; I will even deal with thee as thou hast done, which hast despised the oath in breaking the covenant. *Nevertheless* I will remember my covenant with thee in the days of thy youth, and I will establish unto thee an everlasting covenant. (Ezek. xvi. 59 – 60.)

Yet also I lifted up my hand unto them in the wilderness . . . because they despised my judgments and walked not in my statutes, but polluted my sabbaths: for their heart went after their idols. *Nevertheless* mine eye spared them from destroying them, neither did I make an end of them in the wilderness.
(Ezek. xx. 15 – 18.)

Yet many years didst thou forbear them, and testifiedst against them by thy spirit in thy prophets: yet would they not give ear: therefore gavest thou them into the hand of the people of the lands. *Nevertheless* for thy great mercies' sake thou didst not utterly consume them nor forsake them: for thou art a gracious and merciful God . . . the great, the mighty and the terrible who keepest covenant and mercy. (Nehem. ix. 30 – 2.)

For a small moment have I forsaken thee; *but* with great mercies will I gather thee. In a little wrath I hid my face from thee for a moment; *but* with everlasting kindness will I have mercy on thee, saith the Lord thy Redeemer.
(Isa. liv. 7 – 8.)

And God saw that the wickedness of men was great in the earth, and that every imagination of the thoughts of his heart was only evil continually. And it repented the Lord that he had made man on the earth. . . . And the Lord said, I will destroy man. . . . *But* Noah found grace in the eyes of the Lord.

(Gen. vi. 5 – 8.)

For Israel, then, the redemptive process which has been at work in history from the beginning throbs with this two-beat rhythm. God confronts man with forgiveness through judgment, love through wrath, gospel through law. His proper work is made effective through his alien work; which means redemption through enslavement, homecoming through exile, renewal through destruction, resurrection through death.[1]

Paradoxical though this is, it is gospel, the good news of God's redeeming grace. Its very polarity is a serious call for man's response in penitence, gratitude and the new life of faith. But, plainly, it is inconclusive. Though God's 'nevertheless' is heartening to guilty men, the disheartening question remains: will human history always be incomplete; will it never reach its purposed goal with humanity's full and consistent response to the holy will of God? The ding-dong struggle between the forces of light and the forces of darkness on the battlefield of every human heart throughout historic time – 'there's no end to it!', as we say in moods of vexation or gloom. But ought there not to be an end some day, a triumphant, final vindication of God's redeeming righteousness, when history will reach a climax or goal, and the purpose of God therein will be conclusively exhibited, and God's last word spoken: when (if we may press *The Lost Chord* into the service of theology) the two-beat rhythm will be finally resolved into 'one chord of music like the sound of a great Amen'?

This hope, implicit in prophecy from the beginning, becomes explicit in the later form of prophecy called apocalypse.[2] Here Israel's understanding of history is dominated by eschatology, a doctrine affirming an End which will be the conclusive manifestation and achievement of God's purpose in history.

In principle, apocalypse adds nothing new to prophecy. It is

[1] Cf. Isa. xxviii. 21, and the preceding *vv.* 14 – 18.

[2] Its sole representative in the Old Testament canon is the book of Daniel.

a dramatic and sometimes extravagantly precise statement of the prophetic view of history. Its relation to prophecy is not unlike that of 'cinerama' to the flat screen: no new kinematic principles are involved but the picture has a stereoscopic vividness. Like the prophets, the writers of apocalypses realize that faith in the living God who acts redemptively in history must have an eschatological reference, since it necessarily concerns the climax and final meaning of history. If God is lord of history its ultimate issue must express his purpose. As Dr J. A. T. Robinson has put it (with a neatly ambiguous use of the adverb), 'What is ultimately real must be ultimately realized'.[1] Whereas for the Aryan tradition of Hellenism and philosophical Hinduism 'the essential is what is true timelessly', for the Hebraic-Christian tradition 'the essential is what holds true at the end of time'. In the Bible, therefore, goal and end, τέλος and finis, are equated. It is the end of history, rather than a timeless eternity beyond history, which expresses the complete and perfect will of God. Thus the redeeming activity of the Eternal within time is promissory evidence of that End. Exodus and Sinai, and the strangely shameful and glorious story of the people of God which proceeds therefrom, prefigure the final consummation of the redemptive process – the coming of the Messiah, the Day of the Lord, the ending of the old world order, and the new creation of the new order, which is the kingdom of God. This was the 'consolation of Israel' which prophets and kings desired to see, and for which Jewish piety looked and waited. The details of this consummation were variously conceived, but they expressed one and the same controlling idea: the expectant messianic faith that *in the end* the God of Israel would visit and redeem his people.

But the distinctive fact here is that Israel has always been waiting thus for the Coming One; and she still waits. For the Jews, the Messiah is still to come. To speak in contradictories, they are still in that holy Temple which was brought to an end in the fulness of time. For, by one of the most ironic juxtapositions of history, the Roman armies of A.D. 70 were destroying this symbol

[1] *In the End, God . . .* (James Clarke, 1950), p. 36.

of the old Israel at the very time when the Church of the new Israel was baptizing the Roman empire itself into Christ.

III

The conviction which is the very basis and *raison d'être* of the New Testament is that the Messiah has come; that God has indeed visited and redeemed his people in the action and passion of this Man; that the purposed end of history has here been disclosed with power and great glory. Christians even owe their historic name[1] to their conviction that the Christ is Jesus. He is the consummation of the redemptive process at work in history. In him the kingdom of God has become a reality on earth. 'Christianity' may be said to begin with the new and distinctive confession,

Mine eyes have seen thy salvation which thou hast prepared in the presence of all peoples; a light for revelation to the Gentiles and for glory to thy people Israel. (Luke ii. 30 – 2.)

Whereas the Jew still looks and waits for the Coming One, the Christian asserts that he has already come. This vital difference begins to emerge with the question addressed to Jesus by the disciples of John:

Are you he who is to come, or shall we look for another? And Jesus answered them, Go and tell John what you hear and see: the blind receive their sight and the lame walk, lepers are cleansed and the deaf hear, and the dead are raised up, and the poor have good news preached to them. And blessed is he who takes no offence at me. (Matt. xi. 3 – 6.)

For the full scriptural and Christian understanding of time, then, the gospel takes us beyond the courts of the Temple into the holiest place itself. Here we are on our knees in thanksgiving and adoration before One who is not only the eternally Real and not only the divine Law of righteousness which judges and renews, but God's presence and his very self in this world of suffering, sin and death. Here is a human life and death manifesting, perfectly, representatively and conclusively, that complete obedience to the will of God which is the goal and end of humanity in time. In the words of the New Testament scholar who has done

[1] Acts xi. 26.

14

most to recover for us this 'realized' eschatology, 'that beyond which nothing can happen has already happened'.[1] It is what is meant by 'the fulness of time'. Here our primary concern is not with contemplative participation in the eternally real, nor with the effort of our wavering will to do the will of God, but with final revelation in the person and work, the passion and victory of the God-Man. Here we are on our knees because here is One, the only One, who is able to enter within the veil and to stand for ever as our High Priest.[2] We come here and kneel here only *in* him. In him deity itself calls saying 'Come unto me'; and in him humanity answers saying 'Lo I have come . . . to do thy will, O God'.

We have already noticed that for the biblical understanding of time, what is ultimately real must be finally realized. Jesus the Christ is that final, conclusive realization. Here *is* the kingdom of God. Here the end of history has come upon men, because the vicarious and representative work of redemptive obedience given to Christ to do – is finished (John xix. 30).

As it was axiomatic for Israel that the era of the Spirit would have come when this happened, it is not surprising that Spirit is the inclusive atmosphere of New Testament thought. The Acts of the Apostles is a book dominated by the fact of the Spirit, and of the signs which accompany, manifest and interpret its creative activity. The Church, the new community of the Spirit, is in-dubitable proof of the presence of the age to come, the era of the Messiah. This presence of the Spirit in power authenticates the gospel of the new age, since it is the constitutive sign and reality of the new age. Christians are people who are already tasting of its powers.

Thirty years ago, when I was learning the history of Christian doctrine at Oxford by the time-honoured method of teaching it, I received much kindness from the Master of University College, Sir Michael Sadler. And I well remember the animation of his handsome features as he greeted me one afternoon, early in the

---

[1] C. H. Dodd.
[2] Heb. x. 19 – 22. Cf. p. 57, below.

Michaelmas term, and began to tell me of a recent, unique experience. He had come from Switzerland. Voice and eye betraye his emotion as he spoke of a remarkable man there to whom h had been listening the previous week. 'His name was Barth Karl Barth, I think it was; have you ever heard of him? . . You see, . . . he made me feel that to-morrow had already hap pened.'

Sir Michael Sadler was not a theologian, and we may assum that he had not so much as heard of 'realized' eschatology in 192ς But through the preaching of the Word, the Spirit had newl convinced him of that finality of God's deed in Christ which ι the purposed end of all history. The preached word of the gospε had made him freshly aware that this unambiguously historicα figure, crucified under Pontius Pilate, is the expected figure ς eschatology: that in Christ all time, past and future, discloses an conveys its final, divine meaning.

But is this realized eschatology convincing? Not altogetheı The great irrelevance of Christianity is that its declarations seen utterly refuted by facts. Its gospel of the new world looks con temptibly meaningless in a world of sin and shame which hε given it the lie from the first. This is a stumbling-block not onlγ to Jews but to many modern Christians; and it ought to bε When the Jew objects that nothing of what he expects to happeι in the messianic age has actually happened, it is very hard fo the Christian to answer him. This formidable difficulty is familiaı but its statement comes with special force from one of the leadinξ thinkers of our age, Paul Tillich, since his exposition and defenc of Christianity is centred in just this 'new being' or new realitγ which has come into the world with Christ. Asking the olε divisive question 'Has the Messiah come?', he says:

What, for instance, *can* we answer when our children ask us about the child iι the manger while in some parts of the world all children 'from two years olε and under' have died and are dying, not by an order of Herod, but by thε ever-increasing cruelty of war and its results in the Christian era, and by thε decrease in the power of imagination in the Christian people? Or, what can w answer the Jews when the remnants of the Jewish people, returning froι eath-camps, worse than anything in Babylon, cannot find a resting place anywhere on the surface of the earth, and certainly not among the great Christian nations? Or, what can we answer Christians and non-Christians who have realized that the fruit of centuries of Christian technical and social civilisation is the imminent threat of a complete and universal self-destruction of humanity? And what answer can we give to ourselves when we look at the unhealed and unsaved stage of our own lives after the message of healing and salvation has been heard at every Christmas for almost two thousand years?[1]

It is difficult, therefore, for modern man to be thrilled by the messianic faith aroused when Jesus came into Galilee declaring that the promises were being fulfilled, that the decisive hour was even then striking, that the end was already happening, and that God was even then acting with decisive finality to redeem the world. To many, indeed, it seems oddly perverse to contend that we are now living in a redeemed world; that is, a world *different* from the world before Christ in that it is penetrated by 'the powers of the age to come'.

And yet, the Christendom of nineteen centuries has been made and sustained by this very eschatological faith which it has so consistently corrupted. 'He made me feel that to-morrow had already happened.' Sir Michael Sadler was referring to Barth; but Barth's reference here would be to the Holy Spirit, for it was the self-authenticating experience of the Spirit which made men feel it at Pentecost, and has made them feel it ever since. At Pentecost fifty days after Easter, it became abundantly convincing. It is instructive to notice that the fourth gospel represents the other tradition according to which the gift of the Spirit is the immediate sequel and effective sign of the Resurrection. This would seem to mean that divergent traditions linked the Spirit's outpouring with Easter and Pentecost respectively. But is there any significant divergence? Both traditions attest the one reality which matters, namely that the Spirit, *the* effective sign of the new creation, is the risen Lord at work in the imperishable community of his Body. As St Paul put it explicitly in one place, 'The Lord is the Spirit'.[2] Through the Spirit at Pentecost the

[1] *The New Being* (S.C.M. 1956), p. 94.
[2] II Cor. iii. 17.

kingdom of God became convincing. The adjective is apt, for in the fourth gospel the Spirit is called 'Paraclete', a word which meant 'convincer' as well as 'comforter'. The New Testament is saying that he, the Lord, the Spirit, makes us feel that the End which is the kingdom of God, has already come upon men. 'We are in a world', wrote Forsyth, 'which has been redeemed; and not in one which is being redeemed at a pace varying with the world's thought and progress.'

It is plain, then, that the Christian concept of the fulness of time compels us to face a difficulty so formidable as to be almost heart-breaking. Yet it is a difficulty which measures the magnitude of the problem of man's redemption, and allows us to remember for our comfort that the Church has lived with this problem from the beginning. For it is the candid paradoxical witness of the Church in its earliest age that the End which is realized in Christ is, in another sense, not yet realized. We still sin and suffer, we still have to die. Satan has fallen as lightning from the court of heaven, but he still 'goeth about as a roaring lion seeking whom he may devour'. We see Jesus crowned with glory and honour, but 'not yet are all things put under him'. The blessedness of the messianic age experienced by the first Christians is always tense with this antinomy. This dual emphasis is found throughout the New Testament where the great gifts of God are present possessions yet objects of hope. Just as St Paul speaks of our justification by faith as a present reality and a future event,[1] so the eschatology of the New Testament as a whole is 'futurist' as well as 'realized'. The End which is already here is 'not yet'. Christ's advent itself is twofold, a *geminus adventus* – his coming in humiliation and his future coming in glory. The Spirit itself which 'realizes' the messianic age and is its effective sign, is also described as a ἀρραβών, the earnest or sample guaranteeing that the main consignment, yet to come, will be of the same kind and quality. In modern Greek the word means 'engagement ring' – the proleptic realization of that which is nevertheless 'not yet'.

[1] Gal. ii. 17, v. 5, Rom. iii. 13.

In cynical mood we may want to dismiss this as perverse; a fool attempt to have the fulness of time both ways: present yet future; here yet not here; yes and yet no. But this dialectical ambiguity has played too big and enduring a role throughout three thousand years of our religious history to be so dismissed. It has been called 'the telescoping of time', and cumbrously analysed as 'the transcendence of temporal limitation', or as 'the sense of contemporaneity', or as 'unsere Gleichzeitigkeit mit Christus': and, as the discussion of the sacraments of baptism and eucharist towards the close of this book will seek to show, it is only in Christian worship, where religion has the wholeness that belongs to life, that such analysis yields to synthesis, and tense distinctions are dissolved, and the redeeming action of the eternal God in the fulness of past time is a present reality.

Real religion presupposes and makes actual the abiding philosophical mystery of eternity and time. The gospel of our redemption declares that the eternal God was in the Man Christ Jesus reconciling the world unto himself. The chapters which follow seek to understand and interpret that gospel in terms of victory, sacrifice and judgment – the threefold imagery which holy scripture uses of the Cross.

CHAPTER II

CHRIST'S VICTORY OVER SATAN

Suffering, sin and death are shadows which darken every huma[n] life. What are we to make of this evil in the world? The Greek[s] asked 'Whence is evil?', and it is humanity's oldest problem. [St] Augustine stated it with his usual succinctness: 'Either God car[n]not abolish evil or he will not. If he will not is he good? If h[e] cannot is he God?'

I

The great monistic systems come to terms with this problem b[y] putting evil in inverted commas, as it were. They deny that it ha[s] any positive ontological standing; it is not real in any ultima[te] sense. Indian philosophy, for example, is predominantly monist[ic] in that it regards the world of sense and plurality, the phenomen[al] world of our everyday knowledge, as unreal and illusory. Th[e] only real knowledge is knowledge of Brahman; but this is h[is] own knowledge of himself, since the subject in the act of knowin[g] is identified with him. The whole world, with all its discorda[nt] particularities, is thus resolved into Brahman.

> They reckon ill who leave me out;
> When me they fly I am the wings.
> I am the doubter and the doubt,
> And I the hymn the Brahman sings.

On such ontological presuppositions evil is an illusion d[ue] to our finitude. Spinoza, the great Western monist, called [it] 'darkness in us'. And did not the Oxford Hegelian F. H. Bradle[y] maintain that there is no pain 'on the whole'? He meant that ju[st] as in an elaborate machine the pressures and resistances of th[e] several parts subserve an end beyond any one of them, so th[e] seeming distinctions and contrarieties of experience are transcended in the ineffable unity of the Absolute.

> Far or forgot to me is near,
> Shadow and sunlight are the same.
> The vanished gods to me appear
> And one to me are shame and fame.

For thoroughgoing monism, good and evil are alike, in that they are mere appearances (albeit necessary) of the One who transcends both.

For the great dualistic systems, on the other hand, evil is scandalously and inexpugnably real. The sovereignty of God is therefore nominal rather than actual and effective. He is not really master of the cosmic household. As goodness and light he is doing his best against an opposing principle of evil and darkness. An anti-god fights with him. Our world is therefore a battle-field, and we are the unhappy victims of the war of liberation. Manichean dualism, enunciated by Mani seventeen centuries ago, is thoroughgoing; evil is a positive, self-subsistent principle; the No implicit in the primal Yes. Zoroastrian dualism, a few centuries older, is less thoroughgoing because the Persians, though an Aryan people, were aware of the historical, and thought in terms of eschatology. Evil, though real, is less powerful than the good; the god of goodness and light will ultimately triumph, and true religion is response to a bracing moral call to join in the fight, and in the final victory.

There, then, is the contrast, writ large in the history of religion. Speaking broadly, it is the contrast between the religious man's metaphysical sense and his moral sense. Do not the philosophers tend to be monists, and the prophets dualists? As Dean Inge dryly observed, 'The notion of a finite god is one which the moralist can never afford to forget, or the metaphysician to remember'.

The tragic poets, too, are involved in this contrast. In his *Greek Tragedy* Professor Kitto argues that the transcendental philosophers from Plato onwards have never been at ease with the tragic poets, 'for the philosopher must explain his universe, but the tragic poet knows that it cannot be explained. . . . The flaw in the universe, which the philosophers will have none of, is plain enough to Aeschylus'.[1] Kitto means that the dramatic situation in the *Suppliants* or the *Oresteia* is one of tragic tension. Its complexity is inherent – Artemis against Aphrodite, which seems to mean the divine divided against itself: or Athene resisting the Furies, which implies that reconciling mercy and inexorable justice strive together, as it were within the very breast of Zeus. The antinomy is irresolvable by the intellect. But, says Kitto, Aeschylus never pretended that life was easy, or that Zeus was simple, or that only the guilty are tortured. Does he mean that poets rather than philosophers have been most acutely aware of the suffering of the innocent in this world?

Here we think inevitably of God's servant Job, or of the Suffering Servant of Isaiah liii. We remember Glaucon's prophecy of the fate of the just man: 'In such a situation he will be scourged, racked, fettered; will have his eyes put out; and, at last, after suffering every kind of torture, will be crucified.'[2] In short, we remember that the Messiah himself was crucified; and so we turn to the Bible and to what it says about evil as demonic, and about that divine victory over Satan which is one classic aspect of our redemption.

II

The Hebrews were monotheists. All is of God. He alone creates, sustains and orders all that is. The conception of secondary causes is almost entirely absent from the Old Testament. Isaiah xlv is a superb monument to the prophetic awareness of God's sole causality and governance. 'I am the Lord and there is none else.... I form light and create darkness. I make peace and create evil. I the Lord do all these things.' That tremendous seventh verse reminds us, however, that these monotheists were realists; they did not shut their eyes to the evil in God's universe. Their canon of sacred scripture opens thus: 'God saw everything that he had made and, behold, it was very good' (Gen. i. 31). But its record is soon different: 'God saw that the wickedness of man was great

---

[1] *Greek Tragedy: A Literary Study* (Doubleday, New York, 1954), pp. 10, 21 f., 132.
[2] Plato, *Republic*, ii, 362.

in the earth, and that every imagination of the thoughts of his heart was only evil continually' (Gen. vi. 5).

The Old Testament never evades this mystery of moral evil. Further, it constantly recognizes that nature reflects and shares in sinful man's estrangement from God; nature is no garden of Eden. Further, the animal world contains strange and sinister elements, a fringe of recalcitrance, which has somehow escaped the control of the divine holiness.[1] Even in Noah's ark, where every living thing of all flesh enters two by two,[2] some are called unclean; a difference which the Levitical code does not allow Israel to ignore. Further, the wolf does not lie down with the lamb, nor does the lion eat straw like the ox, nor may the weaned child put his hand on the adder's den. All this is part of the hurt and destruction in God's holy mountain. The eschatology which pervades the scriptures – its very contrast between this age and the age of messianic redemption which is to come – indicates that 'not yet are all things put under him'.

We should not fail to notice, in passing, that it is our own awareness of unending conflict within the natural order which gives to this Hebraic realism its modern relevance. The Hebrews were not specially distinguished above other peoples of antiquity for humaneness[3] or idealism; they were neither strangers to conflict nor shocked by it; and they were not vegetarians. The foregoing evidence from the Old Testament has the more striking kinship, therefore, with Huxley's indictment of nature in his Romanes lecture, and with what modern investigators tell us about the life of fish and other sea-creatures as a vast conjugation of the verb 'to eat'. To complain that 'every prospect pleases and only man is vile' is to over-simplify the problem of evil by ignoring the evil in an order of nature which God saw to be very good. In nature, not only is 'the butterfly killed by the swallow, the swallow speared by the shrike', but the cattle and the rabbits

---

[1] See G. B. Caird, *Principalities and Powers* (Oxford, 1956), pp. 57, 59.

[2] In his play *Noah*, André Obey supplements the biblical story by making the fish swim alongside the ark, in pairs!

[3] Exod. xxiii. 19 and Deut. xxv. 4 notwithstanding.

contend for the grass which is their food, and the roots of the grass struggle ceaselessly with the roots of the trees for survival. When the grass has overcome the fruit trees, shall it be fescue or timothy that lives? When the fruit trees shade grassless earth, which tree's roots shall drain away the moisture from the roots of its neighbour? Admittedly, the use of words such as 'contend', 'struggle' and 'overcome' in this context is dubious because it is anthropomorphic: science warns us against the sympathetic fallacy of seeing nature in our own image, and assuming that the subhuman creation must experience evil where and as we do. The facts are there, however.

> . . . as the gor-crow treats
> The bramble-finch, so treats the finch the moth.

And though we must not attribute actual cruelty to 'Tyger, Tyger, burning bright', a creature predatory by nature, it is hard to resist the thought that its nature is expressive of cruelty which is somehow part of the power which made it what it is. 'Did He that made the lamb make thee?' Is the demonic part of the divine? To put this otherwise, is there some demonic principle which challenges the divine sovereignty by participating parasitically in its creative power, distorting and negating it?

The Old Testament certainly makes use of a crudely dramatic illustration of the demonic challenge to God's sovereignty over nature and man, the ancient Babylonian myth or hymn of creation, which tells how in the beginning the god Marduk fought and killed the ocean dragon Tiamat, an embodiment of the primeval watery chaos, and then created heaven and earth by splitting her huge carcass into two halves.[1] This is rationalized or demythologized almost beyond recognition in Genesis i, but Tiamat still appears in the Old Testament under the names of Rahab, Leviathan and Tehom Rabbah (the great Deep). Prophets and psalmists use this myth not only to recall the dividing of the waters by the firmament at the Creation, but also to recall Israel's greatest historic moment – her exodus from slavery, her deliverance from Pharaoh at the sea. Consider these verses in Ps. lxxiv:

[1] J. G. Frazer, *The Golden Bough*: 'The Dying God', p. 105.

God my king is from of old
  Working salvation in the midst of the earth.
Thou didst divide the sea by thy might;
  Thou didst break the heads of the dragons on the waters.
Thou didst crush the heads of Leviathan.

It is a description of Israel's salvation in terms of God's victory over the monstrous Dragon. The same double victory of God is seen by the prophet as Israel's, and man's, hope of final deliverance:

Awake, awake, put on strength O arm of the Lord;
  Awake as in days of old, the generations of long ago.
Was it not thou that didst cut Rahab in pieces,
  That didst pierce the Dragon?
Was it not thou that didst dry up the sea,
  The waters of the Great Deep?   (Isa. li. 9, 10.)

This became the form of the biblical expectation that God would achieve a final victory over that 'reservoir of all evil',[1] the Ocean Dragon.

In that day the Lord . . . will punish Leviathan, the fleeing serpent, Leviathan the twisting serpent; and he will slay the dragon that is in the sea.   (Isa. xxvii. 1.)

It is illuminating to look further at this in the wider setting of ancient religion. Common to the peoples of the ancient world of the Eastern Mediterranean, the Nile and the Euphrates was a religious mythology which found expression in a more or less uniform religious ritual. The ritual was embedded in annual New Year festivals, its due performance being regarded as essential to man's life and well-being. The role played in this cultus by the king was of great significance and importance. The king-mysticism of the ancient world made it a twofold role: human and divine. The king was the representative or substitute of his people. He was also the representative and 'son' of the god.

It is now beyond controversy that some forms of Israel's worship were influenced by and an expression of this widespread ritual pattern, especially that of the Egyptians and Babylonians. Modern oriental scholars have shown conclusively that remnants of it survive in the literature of the Old Testament, notably in the Royal or Enthronement psalms.

Surveying the Greek mythology of Hesiod's *Theogony*, and

[1] Caird, *op. cit.* p. 62.

25

finding there the same ritual basis, the late Professor F. M. Cornford[1] concluded that

the work of creation is the exploit of a personal god – Marduk, Jahweh, Zeus – who can bring light out of darkness, order out of formlessness, only by first triumphing over the powers of evil and disorder embodied in the dragon of the waters and her brood of monsters. . . . It is now certainly established that the killing of Leviathan by Jahweh or of Tiamat by Marduk was not what Frazer called a 'quaint fancy' of primitive and problematical savages, sitting round the fire and speculating on the origin of the world. . . . Biblical students[2] have made out that the Psalms celebrating it belong to a group of liturgical songs which were recited as part of the Temple worship, at the Feast of Tabernacles. This feast inaugurated the New Year; and in its dramatic ritual the events these Psalms describe were annually re-enacted.

It is inferred from the Psalms that the fight with the Dragon was one episode in the drama, in which, as throughout the festival, the part of Jahweh was taken by the king. There was also a triumphal procession, conducting the divine king in his chariot up the hill of Zion to be enthroned in the Temple. Emblems of new vegetation, fertility and moisture were carried and waved as a charm to secure a sufficiency of rain for the coming year. There are also signs that, at some point in the king's progress, there was another ritual combat. The procession was assailed by the powers of darkness and death, who are also the enemies of Israel, the kings of the earth who took counsel together against the Lord's anointed. The god who wields the thunder intervened to save his royal son and to dash his enemies to pieces. . . .

So the central figure in the New Year rites was the rain-maker, the divine king. But at the advanced stage of civilization we are now considering in Babylon, Egypt and Palestine, the king has become much more than a rain-making magician. To control the rain is to control the procession of the seasons and their powers of drought and moisture, heat and cold; and these again are linked with the orderly revolutions of sun, moon and stars. The king is thus regarded as the living embodiment of the god who instituted this natural order and must perpetually renew and maintain its functioning for the benefit of man. The king embodies that power and also the life-force of his people, concentrated in his official person. He is the maintainer of the social order; and the prosperity of the nation depends upon his righteousness, the Hebrew *Sedek*, the Greek δίκη. He protects his people from the evil powers of death and disorder, as well as leading them in war to victory over their enemies. . . . The rites are regarded as an annual re-enactment of Creation.

[1] *The Unwritten Philosophy and other Essays* (Cambridge, 1950), pp. 105, 108 – 9.

[2] Professor Cornford here referred to the work of Professor W. E. O. Oesterley in *Myth and Ritual* and of Professor A. R. Johnson in *The Labyrinth*. See also the latter's work on the 'Royal' psalms in his *Sacral Kingship in Ancient Israel*. The much debated issue of 'cultic patternism' in the Old Testament is surveyed in *The Old Testament and Modern Study*, ed. H. H. Rowley (1951) and in H. F. Hahn's *The Old Testament in Modern Research* (S.C.M.). There are more detailed studies in Helmer Ringgren's *The Messiah in the Old Testament*, Widengren's *Sakrales Königtum im A.T. und im Judentum* (1955) and S. H. Hooke's *The Siege Perilous* (1956).

The Old Testament, then, witnesses through varied liturgical rites and mythical imagery of great antiquity to evils in man's lot which affront and menace the divine sovereignty, and which cry out for the divine redemption of the whole natural and social order. Among them are the principalities and powers of darkness and death. The references to death in the Old Testament are starkly realistic. The darkness of death, the silence and dust of the grave, are surely an affront to him who is the god of the living. Death, therefore, is *the* enemy to be overcome in God's final act of salvation: that re-creation which will be new creation because it will repeat, and so 'realize', the primal glory of creation itself. As St Paul, a Hebrew of the Hebrews, was to think of it, God had given sinful humanity over to the sway of sinister powers of which Death was the supreme manifestation. For St Paul, therefore, 'the last enemy to be destroyed is Death'. And so we come to the New Testament.

During the past fifty years we have been rediscovering that the New Testament is not really intelligible apart from its 'demonic' presuppositions. In 1909 Dibelius wrote *Die Geisterwelt im Glauben des Paulus* (Paul's belief in the spirit-world), and thus did for the witness to Satan in those earliest writings of the New Testament what Schweitzer had done for the apocalyptic eschatology of the gospels. That is, he showed that it might not be soft-pedalled or ignored merely because it was strange and embarrassing to the theological liberalism of the day. In 1930 Aulén's *Christus Victor* did the same for that dramatic conception of Christ's redeeming work – the divine victory over the devil – which, though dominant in Christendom during the thousand years before Anselm, and strikingly reaffirmed by Luther, was thereafter virtually repudiated and lost by the West until F. D. Maurice and others began to recover it. Aulén's important, though one-sided, thesis found corroborative illustration the following year in Obendiek's *Der Teufel bei Martin Luther*; and in 1935 this theme of God's redeeming victory became impassioned apologetic in Karl Heim's *Jesus der Herr*, where the section on satanic power in the thought of Jesus (*die satanische Macht im Weltbild Jesu*) was followed by an attempt to expound the satanic (*das Wesen des Satanischen*) for a divided modern world heading fast for self-destruction. Written for non-specialists this was less technical (and perhaps more intelligible) than Tillich's profound *Das Dämonische* which had appeared in 1926 – an anticipation of his many masterly contributions to the philosophy of history. But Heim's volume, and its sequel *Jesus als Weltvollender* (Jesus as the world's fulfilment) which appeared in 1937, prepared us for the two notable studies on this subject in the post-war period. Ragnar Leivestad's *Christ the Conqueror*, published in English in 1955, is a comprehensive survey of the manifold New Testament witness to cosmic intelligences and demonic powers, and of their subjugation by Christ, the strong Son of God. But though I owe much to it and to the other writings which I have cited, my paramount debt is to Professor G. B. Caird's *Principalities and Powers*, published in 1956. Though on a smaller scale than Leivestad's volume, it is one of the most discerning and distinguished contributions to biblical and Pauline theology of recent years.

So much for modern research. Its inescapable verdict is that the belief in sinister powers permeates the gospels. This belief is dominant in the earliest, St Mark, where the ministry of Jesus as the Christ, the strong Son of God, is a battle against Satan. The gospel story begins with the mysterious statement that he was in the wilderness forty days, tempted of the devil. Its developing theme is that into our world, dominated by satanic forces, there has come One who is stronger than Beelzebub, the prince of the devils. Its explicit testimony is that the Redeemer's power is, like his authority, divine. It extends not only over the demons – the dark, cosmic forces symbolized in the Temptation, and exercising their power in disease – but over the realm of nature. He stills the tempest, feeds the multitude, walks on water, rides into Jerusalem on an untamed colt.[1] The meaning of these miracles, so difficult for the modern mind, is that here is *the* divine victory

[1] See an illuminating note in Caird *op. cit.* p. 71.

over the Spirit which ever denies (*der Geist der stets verneint*),[1] that cosmic Evil which says No to God's creative and re-creative Yes. They mean that throughout the ministry of Jesus the immemorial ding-dong struggle between the rule of God and the rule of Satan was being fought to its decisive climax, the unique victory of the Cross. From the Temptation onwards that struggle is the context of language such as this:

Didst thou not sow good seed in thy field? Whence then hath it tares? He answered, An enemy hath done this. (Matt. xiii. 27.)

When ye pray, say Our Father ... deliver us from the evil one. (Matt. vi. 13.)

Then entered Satan into Judas named Iscariot. (Luke xxii. 3.)

Simon, Simon, Satan hath desired to have you that he may sift you as wheat, but I have prayed for you. (Luke xxii. 31.)

This is your hour and the power of darkness. (Luke xxii. 53.)

The prince of this world cometh and he hath nothing in me. (John xiv. 30.)

Now is the judgment of this world; now shall the prince of this world be cast out. (John xii. 31.)

I beheld Satan fall as lightning from heaven. (Luke x. 18.)

This language of cosmic struggle permeates St Paul's thought also. It occurs in every epistle except the short letter to Philemon. He says that Satan constantly hinders his work – speaking much as a farmer might speak of the weather. He describes Satan as the god of this world, blinding men's minds; and as the prince of the power of the air. He says that it was the rulers of this aeon, the principalities and powers, who crucified the Lord of glory and, in so doing, over-reached themselves, were despoiled and made a mockery. The reference is not to the outward events and the visible actors of the Jerusalem scene in Holy Week; Paul is not speaking primarily of Pilate, Herod and Caiaphas. Behind that

---

[1] Mephistopheles in *Faust*, Part I; the scene in the *Studierzimmer*.

ostensible action he sees 'the world rulers of this present darkness'.
It is over them that Christ is Victor in the strife.

III

But what is the modern man to make of all this? Fifty years ago,
in the heyday of a complacent liberalism, much theology regarded it with a patronizing smile, if not an embarrassed im-
patience. We hurried away from these dramatic and bizarre
motifs of conflict which are now seen to be a dominating pattern
in the biblical gospel of salvation. As for Satan, he was dismissed
with a joke as fanciful if not crude mythology. There was a
picture in *Punch* which showed two nice little girls playing together, when one asked the other, 'Do you believe in the devil?'
And the reply was, 'Of course not, silly; it's like Santa Claus; it's
only Daddy'. It may be said, of course, that such an attitude is a
very proper disavowal of barbarous nonsense about a devil with
horns, tail and toasting-fork. Christians cannot and do not believe
in an anti-god: they are not ditheists.

But to-day the very elements in the New Testament for which
the confident liberal epoch had little use make a strong appeal to
the imagination because they have a new relevance. In this
twentieth century man's sense of the evil reigning in the world
has again become acute. To Berdyaev, for example, our world is
in the victorious grip of the inane; almost overwhelmed by
meaningless evil. 'Meaninglessness', too, is a key word in Tillich's
analysis of modern existentialism, and he constantly recalls the
witness of modern art, poetry and drama to that permanent contradiction between man's essence and his existence, which is the
inescapable predicament of the sons of Adam. Man as he *exists* is
not what he *essentially* is and ought to be. He is estranged from his
true being. It is part of the meaning of the demonic. Even in that
self-styled era of enlightenment, the eighteenth century, when the
gap between essence and existence was confidently closed, Kant
was to embarrass his contemporaries by his stiff insistence on
'radical evil' (*das radikale Böse*) as part of the constitution of life
as man knows it. We understand what Kant meant. Two world

wars in one generation and the imminent possibility of a third of unimaginable horror make us feel like counters in the hands of invisible, supra-individual, extra-mundane powers – those κοσμοκράτορες, ἄρχοντες and στοιχεῖα spoken of in the New Testament. We no longer feel free in the sense presupposed by kid-gloved idealistic philosophies. We extend our supposed dominion over the powers of nature only to become more tightly tied and bound by their chain. Modern man's atomic science has taught him the truth of Nietzsche's dictum that his culture is ever in danger of destruction by the very instruments of culture.

Is it surprising, then, that modern thinkers in different fields have rediscovered the relevance and force of New Testament demonology? *Screwtape* is more than a brilliant joke. Otto Piper, professor of New Testament at Princeton, is affectionately known as the man who brought the devil back to Princeton, because for twenty years he has been reckoning seriously with concepts which can hardly be eliminated from the New Testament without altering its essential meaning. One of the most eminent of modern church historians, Professor Roland Bainton of Yale, asked in his life of Luther (1950), 'Is God Lord of all, or is he himself impeded by demonic hordes? Such questions a few years ago would have seemed to modern man but relics of medievalism. . . . To-day so much of the sinister has engulfed us that we are prone to wonder . . . .'[1] John Cowper Powys is more explicit:

We westerners are . . . inclined to underrate the possibility in so mysterious a cosmos of invisible forces at work . . . that are powerful ministers of evil. . . . Older races than ours, less 'scientific' no doubt but with a far longer experience in the possibilities of life upon earth, have never lost their sense of vast spiritual conflicts going on about us in which, willy nilly, we have to share. To Dostoievsky this awareness was as vivid as to any white magician in the monasteries of Tibet.[2]

Language so explicit forces the obvious issue. Is it to be taken literally? Or is it mythology, implying nothing more actual than

[1] *Here I Stand: A Life of Martin Luther*, p. 50 (Abingdon Press; Mentor Book edition, 1955).
[2] *The Pleasures of Literature* (Cassell, 1938), p. 222.

is implied by 'John Bull' or 'Father Christmas'? Are we really to believe in that old storm-centre of debate, a personal devil? Or is it more intelligible to repeat Tillich's ontological profundities about non-being eternally present and eternally overcome within being itself (*esse ipsum*)?

> Christian, dost thou see them
>   On the holy ground;
> How the powers of darkness
>   Compass thee around?
> Christian, up and smite them . . . .

Is this effectively dramatized psychology, or are there, as in Thomas Hardy's *The Dynasts*, 'discarnate intelligences', having that *overagainstness* which is involved in independent being? Fear, Discord, Anxiety, Corruption, Pride seem to have such invasive, disintegrating, cunning and enslaving power as to *be* unclean spirits. Are such evils devils; or must Ockham's razor cut off the added initial letter as an illegitimate multiplication of entities?[1]

One thing, at any rate, is now recognized: myth no longer carries a slur. It is not only a legitimate form of human thought; it is an indispensable form, conveying meanings for which the propositional formulas of science and philosophy may be inadequate. It is the only way, as Plato's examples show, in which the supra-sensible can be grasped. Often it is our only way of articulating the paradoxes which religion makes inevitable but which logic leaves irresolvable. With this in mind let us turn back to the biblical paradox of the demonic.

In the Old Testament 'satan' means 'adversary'. The word is a noun, preceded by the definite or indefinite article, before it becomes a proper noun and a name. The foreign kings sent by God against the apostate Solomon are described as 'satans'. The satan, then, means 'the adversary' or 'the accuser'. There is a

---

[1] It is ironical that the famous 'razor' associated with the second founder of nominalism, William of Ockham, is wrongly attributed to him. It occurred first in Condillac, and was used by Sir William Hamilton in 1852. The garbled version, *entia non sunt multiplicanda praeter necessitatem*, was invented by John Ponce of Cork in 1639. See W. M. Thorburn's authoritative discussion in *Mind*, no. 107, July 1918.

story – an apocryphal story – that Calvin's nickname among his fellow-students in Paris was 'the Accusative Case'. The truth with which we are concerned here is that accusation was and is Satan's function. He opposes men in their pretensions to a right standing with God. He does it on God's behalf. It is a divine function. He represents God's trying and sifting justice. As an angel or personification of that divine attribute of justice he is hardly distinguishable from God. Luther's insistence that the devil is always God's devil was soundly biblical (as not everything in the Bible is). As the very Embodiment and Agent of the divine judgment on sin, Satan is the public prosecutor in the heavenly court. As Caird observes, his divine function is to indict sinners at the bar of heaven; he is the greatest of God's law-enforcement officers, the angels of punishment. Without being flippant we may use Gilbert and Sullivan to the glory of God and describe him as God's Lord High Executioner. It is one side of the biblical paradox of Law and Gospel.

But there is another side, where this stern legal emphasis is confronted by its opposite, an evangelical emphasis. The Old Testament provides at least one notorious illustration of it. In II Samuel xxiv God is described as having incited King David to take a census of the people, and then as having punished him for so doing. Now this *may* illustrate what the great Professor A. B. Davidson called 'the particularly conspicuous Old Testament tendency to refer all things back to God'. He cites (as we have already done) Isaiah xlv. 7, and adds I Samuel xvi. 14 and I Kings xxii. 20 f. as illustrations of this Old Testament insistence on God's sole causality. But the notorious passage which evokes this dexterous (or should it be 'sinister'?) exegesis means *prima facie* that God tempts David to do wrong that he may have just cause for his subsequent anger. Obviously he is far from qualifying for the schoolboy's famous tribute to his head master, 'a beast, but a just beast'. And the most illuminating comment on this *crux interpretum* occurs in a later document, I Chronicles xxi, where the same historical event is described differently. Here it is Satan who incites David to the punishable act. Why has the Chronicler altered the earlier text, ascribing temptation to Satan and so tacitly denying it of God?

Caird's discerning answer is that the alteration indicates a growing awareness that the legal and punitive activities which may be ascribed to God's servant Satan are not, in the final issue, worthy of God himself. That is, Satan's activity, though carried out on behalf of God is in some way contrary to God's true nature and his ultimate purpose. The wrath of the Law *is* of God's appointing: it is holy and just and good. But, as Luther was to put it, it is God's *opus alienum* rather than his *opus proprium* (his 'strange work' rather than his 'proper work'). Here, too, Luther was soundly biblical.[1] In the very contradiction between these two accounts of David's census we have an evangelical awareness that law is not the only nor the final truth about God. Satan stands inflexibly for law and for nothing else. He is 'a martinet' who demands that sinful men shall be dealt with according to the law's full rigour. That is, he is so zealous to vindicate God's honour that he will go to any length to secure a verdict of guilty. He is Mr Legality on the cosmic scale. And the point is that if God were nothing more than inexorable legal justice he would be just this: we men being what we are he would be no more than the great Accuser. A division within the divine nature – God's grace *versus* his law; God's mercy *versus* his holiness – is, when stated thus in conceptual terms, an intolerable logical contradiction: but stated in imagery which actualizes the living unity of the contradictory concepts, it becomes the precious evangelical paradox of redemption.

Satan's rebellion and his fall from heaven are a symbolic way of saying the unsayable; namely, that legal rigour both represents God and misrepresents him; that the wrath of God revealed against all unrighteousness is the agent of God's holy purpose and yet the enemy of that purpose. It is this paradox which the biblical figure of Satan illustrates. By insisting exclusively on the law's demands, God's satan becomes the enemy of God's redeeming grace. The dualism, nakedly explicit in the New Testament con-

[1] Isa. xxviii. 14 – 18, 21. This is further discussed in chapter III.

flict between the kingdom of God and the kingdom of Satan, is already disclosed in the Old Testament. With the evangelization of the concept of God's righteousness – a righteousness which redeems as well as judges – there grows the sense of difference and conflict between God and Satan. In the prologue to the book of Job God's tester and judge of men is becoming their tempter; the public prosecutor is on the way to being the *agent-provocateur*[1]. In short, the servant of God is on the verge of rebellion against God, and in the story of the garden of Eden this is open and explicit: Satan has been identified with the Serpent ever since.

As we have already noticed, the climax of the story is Christ's redeeming victory over Satan on the deadly Tree. The New Testament understands redemption as his victory – unique, representative and final – over the powers of evil which make the world of nature and history a waste land. The historical facts of the conflict waged in Judaea in A.D. 29 'under Pontius Pilate' have universal, trans-historical, eternal significance. Christ's adversaries stand for permanent factors in human experience wherein good is distorted and perverted by a deep-seated wrongness and misdirection. Behind the ostensible conflict of that Holy Week is the conflict with principalities and powers, actualized in the Temptation in the wilderness and carried through in the whole process ending in the Cross. The kingdom of evil stultifies itself in assault on One whose whole response to the situation is a pure embodiment of the will of God through obedience unto death. That is the meaning of the words, 'The prince of this world cometh and hath nothing in me'. Further, the creative energies of the will of God incarnate in this Man are recreative: they sweep on through the Cross to the Resurrection. He is Victor. 'The strife is o'er, the battle won.'

We need little reminding, of course, that it is not over; at least, not for us. Christians have still to contend 'against principalities, against powers, against the world rulers of this present darkness' (Eph. vi. 12). That is, Satan is still the Accuser here on

[1] Caird, *op. cit.* pp. 36, 37.

earth even though he be now fallen from heaven. 'Your adversary the devil goeth about as a roaring lion seeking whom he may devour' (I Pet. v. 8). 'The whole world lieth in the evil one' (I John v. 19). In his own conflict Christ was victor, finally and absolutely. Our conflict is not like that because our humanity is sinful, guilty, bound to a dark inheritance and a tainted existence. But what makes Christ's victory Gospel, good news for *us*, is that it was and is on our behalf. The Israel of God is identified with Christ, crucified and risen with him. Indeed, the whole Gospel might be stated in ten short words: God in Christ for us; we in Christ for God. One of the classic ways of saying this in the New Testament is that the accuser of Adam's race has already been cast down by a second Adam.[1] There is therefore now no condemnation to them that are in Christ Jesus; for the law of the spirit of life in Christ Jesus has made them free from Satan's law of sin and death. And so the paradox of the divine, which redeems in condemning and condemns in redeeming, reaches the climax of its mythological expression thus:

And the great dragon was cast out, that old serpent called the Devil and Satan, which deceiveth the whole world. He was cast out into the earth and his angels were cast out with him. And I heard a loud voice saying in heaven, Now is come salvation and strength, and the kingdom of our God, and the power of his Christ. For the accuser of our brethren is cast down which accused them before God day and night. And they overcame him by the blood of the Lamb.   (Rev. xii. 9-11.)

IV

The ultimate meaning of such grotesque apocalyptic imagery is that it dramatizes the antinomy which is inherent in the Christian theology of atonement, and without which that theology cannot be truly expressed.

There are three great biblical metaphors, taken respectively from the battlefield, the altar of sacrifice and the law-court, which seek to describe and explain the action and passion of the

[1] The deliverance has already begun in principle (Luke x. 18f., Col. i. 13, I John iv. 4, John xii. 31, xvi. 11) but it will not be completed till the parousia of Christ (Rom. xvi. 20, I Cor. xv. 26, II Thess. ii).

Cross. They are Christ as Victor; Christ as Victim; Christ as Criminal; and they are later expanded into systematic theories of atonement. All three are attempts to express a paradox which is conceptually inexpressible, namely that here something was done for sinful men – not only *by* God but *to* God.

First something done by God. God was in Christ reconciling the world unto himself. That is, Christ's redeeming work is something initiated and done by God, since his nature and property is ever to have mercy and to forgive. This is his *opus proprium*, his proper activity, the final truth about him. Thanks be to God; this is Gospel, Good News.

Second, something done to God. The New Testament strikes another, complementary note. It speaks unambiguously of the holiness, wrath and judgment of God; it uses the concepts of the payment of a price, the expiation of guilt, the legal penalty for sin. The gospel never says that these concepts express the whole and the ultimate truth about God: it would be no *good* news if it did. But it does say that here is God's *opus alienum*, an activity which is ultimately strange and foreign to his purpose of redeeming love, but which – as holy law, making its terrifying demand on the sinner – is the only background against which redeeming grace can be seen in all its wonder. Did not Kierkegaard observe that no man can really know God as his friend unless he has first known him as his enemy? That God can be both at once – the one who is not mocked, and the one who does not deal with us according to our sin – this is what all these metaphors of atonement are struggling to say.

We must discuss this antinomy of Law and Gospel in the next two chapters where we consider the sacrificial and penal metaphors taken respectively from Altar and Law-court. Here we are concerned with the first of these three metaphors, taken from the battlefield or the slave-market: Christus Victor. And, as we have seen, it contains this same antinomy, that at the Cross something is done by God and to God.

The precise thinker may protest at the contention that the powers overcome by the divine redeemer on the cross are at the

same time divine powers, the ministers of the divine wrath: that
God both pays the ransom and yet receives it; that he loses the
battle and yet wins it: in brief, that redemption is in some sense
an activity of God upon himself. The hymn-book may ask such
a man to sing

> Thou permitt'st, dread Lord, that we
> Take refuge from thyself in thee;

but, if he be philosophically-minded, that is poetic licence rather
than disciplined theology.

I am far from wanting theology to escape from all philosophical discipline. A deliberate flight from reason in the name of
religion can lead to pernicious obscurantism. But, as I have
already argued, so far from being discreditable, the so-called
licence of poetry is often indispensable, even to reason. Is it not
one of the profoundest characteristics of religion that it constantly confronts us with a fusion and interpenetration of elements
which, for our minds, are paradoxical and unreconciled? We
call this an antinomy because it simultaneously admits the truth
of two contrary assertions: they are logically incompatible but
they have an equal ontological necessity. Further, though the
antinomy witnesses to a contradiction impenetrable by the logical
mind, the contradiction is nevertheless actualized and lived in
human experience.

The contradiction between the 'demonic' and the Christian
doctrine of creation is obvious. All is of God who creates, sustains
and orders all things in holy love. Yet the transitoriness of everything created – 'the roar of greedy Acheron' – and the power of
the demonic in the human soul and in history, are facts of experience. That is why these negativities have a decisive place in
biblical religion in spite of its doctrine of creation: they are asserted in spite of the intellectual problem which their assertion
involves. Biblical theology boldly declares a demonic anti-
divine principle which participates nevertheless in the power
of the divine.

Critics have been disturbed by Tillich's admission that there
is 'a point in which creation and the fall coincide, in spite of their

logical difference'.[1] But is not this a dangerous yet inescapable truth of which all theology, Eastern and Western, Catholic and Protestant, has always been aware? Two examples of this awareness will suffice.

First, to the question '*When* did the devil rebel?' medieval scholasticism answered '*statim post creationem*' (immediately after the creation). It was a hair-splitting attempt to safeguard the sole causality of God and the perfection of his creation while admitting the reality of evil which that creation makes logically inconceivable. The words *statim post* are theology's dialectical Yes and No. Tillich makes the same answer by saying that there is no point in time and space in which created goodness was actualized and had existence. 'Actualized creation and estranged existence are identical.' Only those who cling to the literal interpretation of the story of paradise need disagree.

A second example: Luther was vividly aware of this point of coincidence between creation and evil in spite of their logical difference. For him, as much as for St Augustine or Calvin, all is of God. The devil, therefore, is necessarily God's devil. As omnipresent, God is present even in the devil (*selbst im Teufel gegenwärtig*). The devil is God's instrument (*Werkzeug Gottes*). Indeed Luther comes dangerously near to making sin a rational necessity, for he says that since God moves and acts in all that is, he necessarily moves and acts in Satan and sinner (*necessario movet etiam et agit in Satana et impio*). But though for Luther the devil is ever God's instrument, no theologian (not even Gregory of Nyssa) was ever more emphatic that the devil is the enemy of God and man, and that God in Christ has therefore fought and worsted

---

[1] *Systematic Theology*, II, 44 (Chicago), where Tillich discusses this difficulty. We may add that as the Christian doctrine of creation means that the world is from God and perfect, it cannot logically contain a rebellious devil; the perfection which he mars would already be incomplete through his very existence. Further, its perfection would already be incomplete through its *potential* corruptibility. The temptability of Adam is logically incompatible with that original perfection which Christian theology postulates in him. And even if we make use here of Tillich's distinction (*op. cit.* II, 127f.) between 'desire' and 'concupiscence', in order to safeguard the freedom which makes man *man*, it is still logically inconceivable how 'desire' (as implicit in God's creation of human freedom) can become the 'concupiscence' which is its corruption. Given the Christian doctrine of creation in its classic form, not only sin but temptability itself remains a mystery: *posse non peccare* is as baffling as *posse peccare*.

39

him. We have only to look at Luther's vivid Easter hymns, and at his two *Catechisms*, to hear this theme of *Christus Victor* sounding like a trumpet. Admittedly there are downright demonic elements in Luther's doctrine of God (where Blake's *Tyger* merely puts the question), especially in some of his descriptions of God's activity in nature and history. And if they are, as Tillich says, the greatness and the danger in Luther's understanding of the holy,[1] the same is true of many passages in the Psalms, the Prophets, and the book of Job. As for Luther's occasional identification of the wrath of God with Satan, this is explicit or clearly implied in at least four passages of the New Testament itself.[2]

We cannot rest in an unstable equilibrium of Yes and No, of course; and the New Testament itself does not. Its philosophy of history is an eschatology. The dialectical tension is real, and we live in it as we wait for the End. But we live victoriously in it, and we are saved by hope. Our age seems to have forgotten how powerful an experience faith of the dimension which underlies the New Testament can be. The first Christians mean by participation in Christ's victory precisely what the words mean. God is known as the One who giveth us the victory through our Lord Jesus Christ. St Paul, the earliest Christian of whom we have real and extensive knowledge, simply declares: 'I am sure that neither death, nor life, nor angels, nor principalities, nor things present, nor things to come, nor powers, nor height, nor depth, nor anything else in all creation, will be able to separate us from the love of God in Christ Jesus our Lord.'

Words of such astonishing power are the victory that overcometh the world; their very utterance is a definition of faith, and an explanation of its eschatological vision of the final goal of all things. That vision is twofold. First, Christians look and wait for the final consummation when the principalities and powers will be subdued into impotence; it will be the final phase of their defeat. But it will not be God's final word about them. For, in the second place, as St Paul repeatedly insists, Christians

[1] *Op. cit.* I, 217.

[2] I Cor. v. 5, I Pet. v. 8, I John v. 19, I Tim. iii. 6.

look forward to a final restoration of all things, which is reconciliation: the reconciliation of all created being, including the principalities and powers, with him who in the end will be 'all and in all' as in the beginning. Restoration is to be new creation. The goal of the universe is the end of all estrangement, the fulness of reconciliation in Christ. And this will include, not exclude the demonic powers. It means, as even Gregory of Nyssa[1] argued in his *Oratio catechetica* (chapters XXII to XXVI), that Satan himself is finally saved. In the end, though the way of it altogether transcends our knowing and our imagining, the victory of redeeming love will not be an incomplete victory. Even Satan belongs to God, not only at the beginning of his career, but at the end.

[1] I have twice singled out this Cappadocian father of the fourth century because it was mainly in his hands that the theme of *Christus Victor* degenerated crudely into a deceit practised on the devil by God. Like a ravenous fish, the devil gulps down the 'bait' of Christ's flesh only to be caught by the 'hook' of the deity which it covers.

CHAPTER III

CHRIST OUR SACRIFICIAL VICTIM

In our modern world sacrifice has become a mere figure of speech. Parents sacrifice themselves for their children; a politician may sacrifice a career for a principle; on the front page of *The Times* someone is prepared to let me have a mink coat 'at a sacrifice'.

I

In the ancient world sacrifice was no figure of speech but stark fact; the solemn taking and surrendering of the warm blood of life itself; the ritual slaughter of bullock or goat, lamb or pigeon at an altar. It asserted the powerful religious efficacy of shed blood. Ancient man took the necessity of blood-sacrifice for granted. Indeed, sacrifice is as ancient and universal as religion itself; it expresses the ultimate concern of the human race.

But modern man finds the very idea revolting, on more than one ground. Averting the divine displeasure by dashing the blood of an innocent victim against an altar, and sending the smoke from its burning flesh in clouds to heaven, is both morally and aesthetically disgusting. The modern imagination, informed and quickened by modern hygiene, can hardly shut out the nauseating details – stench, flies, the constant ritual manipulating of blood, the septic uncleanness – not only at the ancient sacrificial rock where nomad ancestors had poured out the sacred blood, and at every village altar within the settled community, but also in the famed local sanctuaries, and in the magnificent Temple at Jerusalem which finally displaced them. 'If true worship be spiritual,' argues the sophisticated Western mind, 'how can we bring ourselves to think of it in terms of this immemorial, sacred butchery?'

Such objections now have overwhelming force, even though

they oftern misconceive and misrepresent what Hebraic-Jewish sacrifice was and what it meant. As we must notice later, the sacrificial cultus of Israel may not be interpreted in terms of something categorically different, the forensic ideas of Western criminal law: as though an altar were a place where God's *punishment* of guilty man were transferred to a guiltless animal victim. That would be a pagan caricature of the genius and witness of biblical religion. And, in any case, the context of ideas to which sacrifice belongs is not punitive, but expiatory; it is not juridical but piacular.

But we shall merely fall into an opposite misconception if we suppose that the gospel of Christ crucified has no intrinsic relation to sacrifice. At the heart of that gospel – which originated indubitably with Christ himself, was proclaimed by his first disciples and, in the sacrament of his body and blood, has been the focal centre of Christian worship ever since – are certain concepts of expiation and atonement which are integral to Israel's long tradition of blood-sacrifice. God's saving revelation in Christ cannot be truly understood apart from it.

It was baptized into Christ, admittedly. He nullified the Old Covenant while fulfilling its essential meaning.[1] This does not mean that he explicitly repudiated the Temple cultus of his day; the gospels contain no evidence of such iconoclasm. But they do contain evidence that in one great matter his attitude to tradition was unprecedented and unique. He who saw in his battle with the kingdom of Satan the decisive coming of the kingdom of God knew from the outset that only by dying would he win the victory in that battle. This was revolutionary because it meant the shocking, if not blasphemous, paradox that God's Messiah must suffer and die.

Even if he made no explicit claim to be Messiah, an issue about which modern scholarship is not quite unanimous; and even if pre-Christian evidence for the idea of a suffering and dying Messiah were to be produced, the distinctive fact would remain that Jesus Christ did something for the interpretation of the Old

[1] Jer. xxxi. 31 f.

Testament which had not been done before. He brought together and virtually equated two representative figures in the Old Testament whose functions had hitherto been thought of as separate and different. They are the Son of Man and the suffering Servant of the Lord. The astonishing but decisive thing is that Jesus describes the former in terms of the latter. The Son of Man, who is represented in the book of Daniel as a triumphant figure, is represented by Jesus in the gospels as a figure of sacrifice. The Victor of the Old Testament tradition is both Victor and Victim in the New. It is beyond controversy that as his ministry approached its climax Jesus insisted that the victory of the Son of Man over the principalities and powers had to come through sacrifice and death. St Augustine's characteristic epigram rightly interprets the evidence: *ideo victor quia victima*[1] (he was victor just because he was victim).

It was the Lord himself, then, who declared the necessity and saving significance of his death as a sacrifice for the remission of men's sins. Whether the Last Supper was a Passover-meal or not, this is the plain meaning of a succession of his sayings which reach their climax in the eucharistic words *dēn bisri . . . dēn idhmi* (this my Body . . . this my Blood). To contend that these words had not his death in view is, as Wellhausen himself observed, a bad joke (*ein schlechter Spass*).[2] Jeremias seems right in saying that Jesus is here applying to himself terms from the language of sacrifice. He compares himself with the Passover lamb; he understands his redeeming work on the Cross as a sacrificial offering to the Father, made representatively, on behalf of all humanity.

The inescapable fact is that this perfect offering has always been the beating heart and vital breath of the Church. Here, despite differences and divisions, Christians of all confessions use the same language. It is the language of sacrifice.

> Dear dying lamb, thy precious blood
>   Shall never lose its power
> Till all the ransomed Church of God
>   Be saved to sin no more.

[1] *Confessions* x, 43.
[2] *Das Evangelium Marci* (1903), p. 122.

— William Cowper's words, but I last heard them quoted publicly by a Jesuit. Cowper and Doddridge sing thus in harmony with Bonaventura and Aquinas. Here is the living nerve not only of the Canon of the Mass, but also of the *Hymns for the Use of the People called Methodists*. It is the precious blood, the classic phrase from I Peter i. 19, to which both *Te Deum* and *Rock of Ages* bear witness. The sacred drama which the classic Christian liturgies re-enact, as it were, in *anamnesis*, *eucharistia* and *anaphora* is, in some sense, a paschal drama. 'As often as ye eat this bread and drink this cup ye do show the Lord's death': that is, 'ye do re-enact the drama' of him who was Victor because he was Victim. 'And they sang a new song, saying Thou art worthy to take the book and to open the seals thereof: for thou wast slain, and hast redeemed us (*victor*) to God by thy blood (*victim*), out of every kindred and tongue and people and nation. . . . Worthy is the lamb that was slain'.[1] It is the new song of the unnumbered multitude of the redeemed, standing before the throne of God; and the pertinent fact is that its details would hardly be intelligible apart from the sacrificial rites of the Old Covenant. How, then, are we to understand those rites?

II

We may begin with the famous story about the laconic Calvin Coolidge. Back from church one Sunday in Vermont he was asked for the preacher's theme, and he answered, 'sin'. Just that. Pressed for details he added, 'He was against it'.

There is Israel's, and man's, essential problem. Sin *is* sin, with all its damning guilt upon it. And the eternal God, the holy One who is of purer eyes than to behold iniquity, is against it. If he were not he would not be God. The witness of the Bible is tirelessly explicit here:

How shall I pardon thee for this? Thy children have forsaken me and sworn by them that are no gods. When I had fed them to the full they then committed adultery and assembled themselves by troops in the harlots' houses. They were as fed horses in the morning: every one neighed after his neighbour's wife. Shall I not visit them for these things, saith the Lord, and shall not my soul be avenged on such a nation as this? (Jerem. v. 7 – 9.)

[1] Rom. v. 9, 12.

Your iniquities have separated between you and your God, and your sins have hid his face from you that he will not hear. (Isa. lix. 2.)

Depart from me, ye that work iniquity. (Luke xiii. 27.)

Such indictments abound. But it is also the tireless witness of the Bible that nevertheless[1] Israel is and remains God's people. The relationship between God and his people is a covenant relationship which is inherently indestructible. God loves his people with an everlasting love, in spite of the sinful rebellion which alienates them from him. Though the son becomes a prodigal, he is still a son. The father is still a father even though the far country is the measure of his son's alienation. 'How shall I give thee up, O Ephraim?' Thus, he who is of purer eyes than to behold iniquity ever seeks to mend the broken relationship which it causes.

To use the exact and inevitable adjective, the problem is crucial. How may we believe and declare that God loves and forgives without thereby making light of sin? How can God's grace be free without being 'free and easy'? How can the holiness which must exclude, saying 'Depart from me', be at the same time and in the same situation the love which must include, saying 'Come unto me'? It is this antinomy, this tension between condemnation and forgiveness, between Depart and Come, between No and Yes, between Justice and Mercy, between Law and Grace; it is this contradiction, irresolvable in logic, which was concretely expressed, symbolized and dramatized in the sacrificial cultus of Israel, and which was not only expressed but also resolved, finally and for ever, in the action and passion of the eternal Son upon the Cross.

We touched upon this antinomy in the previous chapter, but we should look at it again, since the three great atonement metaphors of the battlefield, the altar and the law-court are three classic ways in which the Christian faith expresses and resolves it.

In any forgiveness worthy the name – real forgiveness of real wrong – there is always tension, an antinomy irresolvable in logic, between strictness and loving-kindness, between law and

[1] See the discussion of the 'two-beat rhythm' and of the word 'nevertheless' in Chapter I, pp. 10–12.

grace. These polar opposites are not reconcilable in pure thought. But in the stuff of personal relationship, in a concrete instance and act of forgiveness, they *are* reconcilable, because they make a unity. The act of love, for example, in which a faithless husband is forgiven by his wife, or in which a child who has been stealing the housekeeping money is forgiven by his mother, is an act both of exclusion and of inclusion, of rejection and acceptance. For analytical thought there are two distinct realities, the righteousness which judges and the love which seeks; yet the two distinct realities are experienced as one reality. When they fuse, as the effect within us of one and the same personal will, there is forgiveness. As an idea, forgiveness is unconvincing because it is non-moral; but as happening to us in the mystery of personal encounter it is its own evidence. The supreme evidence of it in human history is the Cross. There God's love, which judges and redeems, damns and saves, is experienced fact.[1]

It is this fact, experienced as such at the Cross, which is asserted by the three great atonement metaphors of scripture which have been elaborated in the classic theology of the Church. We have already met one of them. In the preceding chapter we were concerned with the metaphors of rescue or redemption, taken from the battlefield or slave-market:

> A second Adam to the fight,
> And to the rescue came.

Christian theology has used another metaphor, that of justification or acquittal taken from the law-court:

> In my place condemned he stood.

That is, Christ as the criminal; the incarnate and sinless One, 'made sin' on our behalf; so identified with the lost sinners whom he is to seek and save that he is reckoned as one of them. 'He was numbered among the criminals' (Isa. liii. 12, which the Redeemer

---

[1] This paragraph would be incomplete if I failed to add that the analogy implied between human and divine forgiveness is true only up to a point. Tillich (*op. cit.* II, 174) observes that in all human relations he who forgives is himself guilty, not only generally *but in the concrete situation in which he forgives* (italics mine). Human forgiveness should always be mutual therefore.

applies to himself in Luke xxii. 37). The immense paradox of the Christian gospel of forgiveness is nowhere more shocking than in this judicial metaphor. We have to face it in the chapter which follows.

In the present chapter we are concerned with the metaphor of sacrifice, and we must now come to grips with the particular question. What was Jewish sacrifice, and what did it mean?

III

The Romans destroyed the Temple in A.D. 70 and with it the whole Jewish sacrificial system. The complex ritual development of a thousand years was thus ended for ever. One result of this momentous fact was that when the Christian Church came to formulate and standardize its own theology it had ceased to be familiar with animal sacrifice. Almost inevitably, therefore, it misunderstood the original meaning of ritual practices elaborated with such minute precision in the sacred books of its Old Testament. Not until the late nineteenth century did Christian theology as a whole begin to recover the true meaning of sin-offerings in the post-exilic period, or of the special and solemn rite performed for the whole people once a year on the Day of Atonement.

But even so, modern theologians are without an original key to this complicated lock because the ancient biblical records do not provide one. Nowhere do they explain precisely how the sacrificial blood expiated sin, and why it had atoning efficacy. As an established datum, a universally accepted necessity, the altar of sacrifice was its own explanation.

And yet there is a master-key which opens this and all other doors in the house of Israel. The word for it, *b^erith*, is made to sound too much like a legal contract when translated 'covenant', since it means something more intimate and personal; a binding relationship not unlike that symbolized by the wedding-ring. Indeed, for the prophet Hosea, Israel was wedded to Jahweh; *b^erith* meant that she was as closely bound to God as that. From her exodus out of slavery onwards her history was that of his mighty acts of deliverance; it actualized his sovereign grace; at its great moments of crisis and renewal this national consciousness of being the people of God was reaffirmed. The covenant at Sinai itself, expressed in the sprinkling of the sacrificial blood on altar and people, is reaffirmed in the seventh century as the book of Deuteronomy, and again in the post-exilic era as the Priestly Code.

But the point for us is that whereas the covenant relation was dramatically expressed in such high historic moments, it found daily, hourly, almost continuous expression at the altar of sacrifice. Whether the sacrifice was offered publicly or privately, for the individual or for a group; whether it was the appointed rite for Sabbath or New Moon, Feast Day or Passover, it was always a sacramental realization of God's covenant, a means of grace. The settled Jewish system of sacrifice has been called a 'multiplied renewal' of the covenant relation.[1]

The significant word here is 'renewal'. The sacrificial system assumes that man's sin and its correlative, God's wrath, disrupt that right relationship with God which the individual should normally enjoy; and that, before that relationship can be restored, the sin must be 'covered' (an Arabic idiom) by some personal compensatory act, or 'wiped away' (a Babylonian-Assyrian idiom) by some powerful purifying agency. In short, the sacrifice is a sacral act expiating the uncleanness of the sinner and declaring that wrath is not the ultimate truth about God: it is a means of grace which God himself has ordained and provided. The means is blood, the most sacred of all earthly things. It is life itself.

In a normal act of sacrifice for sin in Israel, there were three essential elements:

(i) Because the worshipper is a sinner seeking reconciliation with the holy One who can never condone iniquity, his worship begins with his solemn approach to the altar of God. He 'draws near': a technical term for making an offering. He does not come alone: he comes with his gift, the victim.

(ii) He lays his hand on the head of the victim, thereby effecting the closest possible relation between himself and it: there is some

---

[1] H. Wheeler Robinson, *Redemption and Revelation* (Nisbet, 1942), p. 227.

analogy or correspondence between what is to happen to it and what is to happen to himself. In some sense he is identified with it. We must be cautious about formulating any such rationale of identification however; Eichrodt[1] says that the laying on of the hand (סְמִיכָה) is no more than public testimony to the worshipper's willingness to devote his possessions; and Wheeler Robinson interprets it to mean simply 'this is mine; I give it to thee'. In any case, all our authorities insist that the victim is not thought of as actually substituted for the worshipper; there is no *satisfactio vicaria*. The idea that the victim's life is put in place of its owner's life is nowhere even hinted at.

(iii) He slays the victim, thus releasing its blood which, in accordance with Hebraic psychology, is its life. The priest takes the blood to the altar and smears it upon each of the four horns. Once a year on the Day of Atonement, the High Priest takes it through the veil – the great curtain of purple, scarlet and gold – into the Holy Place. This use of blood expiates sin and effects atonement. Indeed, the one universal and indispensable constituent of sacrifice is blood. Why? Why does all ancient religion agree with Mephistopheles that 'blood is a very special juice' (*Blut ist ein ganz besonderer Saft*)?[2] Does it mean that because the worshipper is now completely identified with the victim, its shed blood symbolizes that he is here surrendering to God the most precious thing he has, his very life? If so, let us not discount it (with a cynical snigger) as a ritual fiction highly convenient for the worshipper. The constitutive and essential element in sacrifice is always the gift, the homage expressed in the act of offering. Here the gift is the most precious of all gifts, life itself. The prescribed method of making it available is an incidental technicality and has no comparable importance (much as the essential meaning of sirloin in the kitchen oven is culinary and nutritive: what happened to the bullock in the slaughter-house beforehand is largely irrelevant).

The main difficulty about a theory of the sacramental identifi-

[1] *Theologie des Alten Testaments* (1933), I, 79.
[2] *Faust*, Part I.

cation of worshipper with victim is that it is nowhere stated in the sources. The great authority of a George Foot Moore, a Pedersen or an Eichrodt is on the whole against this modern spiritualization of ancient realism, because scripture gives it no support; not even in the famous eleventh verse of Leviticus xvii. Indeed, scripture provides no basis for any theory.[1] It seems dangerously easy to import modern, and therefore alien, ideas into an ancient world of symbolic magic, where sin is less a moral offence than a quasi-physical pollution, contracted like an infection; and where the blood of sacrifice is deemed to have a mysterious apotropaic and cathartic power, ridding the sinner of his stain, and so cleansing and sanctifying him.[2] I do not suggest that such elements, common in Arabian, Babylonian and Assyrian rites of exorcism, were much more than environmental survivals in Israel, where the unique and all-important fact was a personal conception of God, and where sin and atonement expressed moral and spiritual relations between persons. But even that word 'survivals' may mislead, since we are not concerned here with two stages in an evolutionary development but with two concentric circles of qualitatively different ideas, represented – as we must notice shortly – by an Amos or a Jeremiah on the one hand and by the book of Leviticus on the other.

Sacrifices were sacraments. As a 'multiplied renewal' of the covenant relation they were effective signs of the Holy One's grace in forgiveness. The wrathful judgment of God is no fiction of a splenetic puritanism; his universe *is* a moral universe. Nevertheless, here is his own means of grace, God's holy ordinance for the restoration of the sinner. Grace means love in action; and here God was not only acting in holy love but taking the initiative. He was not responding to penitence but evoking it. Penitence was essential, of course;[3] all the evidence makes this abundantly clear. Sacrifice presupposed penitence and was its very expression:

---

[1] '*nirgends eine direkte Erklärung*'; Eichrodt, *op. cit.* p. 64.

[2] Art. '*Sacrifice*' by G. F. Moore, *Enc. Biblica*, para. 28 a, p. 4205.

[3] For the moral and religious conditions of atonement through the sacrificial cultus, and the constant insistence on repentance, see *Enc. Biblica*, pp. 4224 – 6.

but sacrifice, as Forsyth put it, is 'the fruit of grace and not its root'. In the Septuagint, where the Hebrew כִּפֶּר (atone) in its various forms is rendered in hundreds of places by ἐξιλάσκεσθαι, in no case is Jahweh the object of the verb. He is always its subject. That is, there is no evidence for a statement or even a hint that God is 'propitiated', as that word is conventionally used. He is always the first mover in the work of reconciliation. All the expiatory praxis whereby the divine Lord of sinful men is to be reconciled with them is of his own initiation and appointment. We should notice that though this is emphasized in the Priestly Code, it is not peculiar to it; it is no post-exilic theologumenon, for it is found throughout Israel's history and even in that of early Babylon. But whereas the magical element pervades Babylonian religion, in Israel it yields to the personal. This means that the heaping-up of sacrifices as *opera operata* is of no avail. Reconciliation depends not on that, but on the obedient acceptance of what the covenant-God has ordained for the maintenance of his covenant. It excludes all calculus of merit, since the whole system of sacrifice proceeds not from man but from God himself.

To sum up thus far: Old Testament sacrifices did not secure God's grace; they declared it and assured men of it without in any way condoning or making light of sin. Sacrifices were not offered to attain God's mercy but to retain it; and to do this, not casually, but with an awed thanksgiving; not with a blasphemous impudence which would take the divine mercy for granted, but with a serious and humble awareness that the divine holiness ever requires that penitence, inward obedience, devotion and self-offering, which are the meaning of true religion.

One vital point must be added. It is still sometimes assumed that the Levitical sacrifices meant penal substitution or vicarious punishment; that is, the substitution of an animal life for a human life justly forfeit; vicarious execution, in short. To this there are insuperable objections.

First: such an idea is quite foreign to the Bible. It is nothing less than pagan to suppose that God will not forgive unless the punishment due to men is visited on innocent animals.

Second: laden vicariously with human guilt, the sacrificial animal would have had to be regarded as polluted and unclean. In fact, however, it was regarded as specially sacred; it could be sacrificed just because and only because it was *not* contaminated by its owner's sin. The popular misuse of the word 'scapegoat' illustrates this persistent misconception. It was precisely the goat sent away into the desert on the Day of Atonement, bearing Israel's sin on its head, which was *not* sacrificed. As we have seen, the use of blood in sacrifice signified expiation of sin by an unblemished and innocent life, offered to and accepted by God.

Third: a very poor man who could not provide any animal might offer a little meal instead. On the assumption that sacrifice meant vicarious punishment, this would have been impossible. You cannot punish a cupful of barley.

Lastly: if this theory (which confuses Temple with Law-court, Altar with Gallows) were true, how came it that no sacrifice was prescribed or allowed for sins committed 'with a high hand'; that is, deliberate and presumptuous sins whose penalty was death? Here no atonement was possible. Sins expiated through sacrifice are just those sins of inadvertence which are not worthy of death.

It is this last point which brings us to a new issue, and so to the New Testament.

The prophetic denunciation of sacrifice is so thorough, frequent and familiar that it needs no detailed illustration.[1]

To what purpose is the multitude of your sacrifices unto me, saith the Lord. I am full of the burnt offerings of rams and the fat of fed beasts: and I delight not in the blood of bullocks, lambs or of he-goats. . . . Bring no more vain oblations. . . . Cease to do evil; learn to do well. . . . Relieve the oppressed.

(Isa. i. 11 f.)

I desired mercy and not sacrifice; and the knowledge of God more than burnt offerings. (Hos. vi. 6.)

[1] Cf. Amos iv. 4, v. 21 f.; Hos. vi. 6, viii. 11 f., xiv. 3 f.; Isa. i. 11 f., xxii. 12 f., xxviii. 7 f.; Jer. vi. 20, vii. 21 – 2; Mic. vi. 6 – 8.

Wherewith shall I approach Jahweh; bow to the exalted God? Shall I approach him with burnt offerings and yearling calves? Will Jahweh accept thousands of rams, myriad streams of oil? Shall I give my firstborn for my transgressions, the child of my body for my own sin?   (Mic. vi. 6 f.)

Comments so devastating can only mean that the theology of sacrifice presents an ideal picture, when all is said, whether we look at the Jerusalem of Isaiah's day, or of the High Priests seven hundred years later. In this fallen world nothing works ideally. The great prophets make it clear that the sacrificial cultus did not move at all times and in all hearts on the high, austere levels of moral realism. They sometimes denied that it was of divine appointment, or that it had any efficacy at all. Did this mean, then, that the sacrifices of the Temple altar became discredited, and that after the attempted Deuteronomic reforms of the seventh century they were soon given up altogether? It did not. The sacrificial cultus continued, not only surviving the exile in Babylon but becoming even more elaborate and formal because of it. Did it mean, then, that the prophetic tradition and the newer priestly tradition represented antithetical strains in the religion of Israel, a pre-Christian illustration of the polar opposition familiar to us as Protestantism and Catholicism (with Anglicanism, like the book of Deuteronomy, making a heartfelt appeal for ambiguity somewhere in between)? It was the facile wisdom of an earlier generation to see such antithesis and opposition here; for the two strains, priestly and prophetic, sacrificial and moral, ritual and personal, were complementary, and deeply interfused. Their obvious parallelism becomes mutual interpenetration in the first and greatest of hymn-books, the Psalter.

O bless our God ye people and make the voice of his praise to be heard. . . .
    I will go into thy house with burnt offerings: I will pay thee my vows
Which my lips have uttered and my mouth hath spoken, when I was in trouble.
    I will offer unto thee burnt sacrifices of fatlings with the incense of rams. . . .
Come and hear, all ye that fear God, and I will declare what he hath done for my soul.   (Ps. lxvi. 8, 12 f.)

I will wash mine hands in innocency: so will I compass thine altar O Lord.
                                    (Ps. xxvi. 6.)

O that men would praise the Lord for his goodness, and for his wonderful works to the children of men. And let them sacrifice the sacrifices of thanksgiving. (Ps. cvii. 21 – 2.)

The intertwining threads of these complementary forms of religious experience in the Psalms illustrate the seriousness of that problem with which we began, namely how to proclaim and give effect to the mercy of God without thereby seeming to make light of sin; how to declare (as one notable Hebrew did come to declare) that 'God justifies the ungodly', without compromising the eternal moral verities. It is the real problem in all forgiveness.

Many Psalms repudiate sacrifices, contrasting an easy *opus operatum* with the right inward disposition of the heart. Personal awareness of a God who punishes sin and forgives it, makes them suspect and renounce what can degenerate easily into a mechanized forgiveness, the correct fulfilment of a legal ordinance.

Sacrifice and offering thou dost not desire; but thou hast given me an open ear: burnt offering and sin offering hast thou not required.
Then said I, Lo I come: in the roll of the book it is written of me. I delight to do thy will, O my God: thy law is within my heart. (Ps. xl. 6 – 7.)

O Lord open thou my lips, and my mouth shall show forth thy praise. For thou desirest not sacrifice, else would I give it: thou delightest not in burnt offering. The Sacrifices of God are a broken spirit: a broken and a contrite heart, O God, thou wilt not despise. (Ps. li. 15 – 17.)

I need not add any comment to a quotation from Psalm li. Not all the Psalms go back on the sacrificial cultus as decisively as this. Some are as near to Leviticus as the fortieth and fifty-first are to Jeremiah. What this means is that the tension remained, and that Judaism could not resolve it effectively.

IV

The corpus of sacred writings which we know as the New Testament is so named because it witnesses to an event in historic time in which the tension was resolved, with convincing finality; when the Old Covenant yields to the New 'once and for all'. That event was the sacrifice of Jesus Christ.

One of these New Testament writings is unique in that it is concerned almost exclusively with our problem. The treatise entitled *To the Hebrews* might be called the Christian synthesis of the prophetic–priestly antithesis, since its concern with perfect sacrifice and eternal priesthood means that here God himself both offers the sacrifice and accepts it.

Let us look at the argument in bare outline. It contrasts the old order with the new order brought into the world by Christ. The priests of the old order, offering the sacrificial blood for sinners, were themselves sinners, doomed like all of us to mortality and its corruption. Further, the sacrifices of the old order were not only imperfect, as their continual repetition showed, but also powerless to deal effectively with sin. If the blood of bulls and goats could not take away the ἀγνοήματα, the sins of ignorance and inadvertence for which it was prescribed, how much less could it deal with presumptuous sin 'done with a high hand'; that is, man's refusal of obedience to the will of God? But there is a new order, a new covenant. Here there is one, sinless priest and one, perfect offering – in which the priest is also the sacrifice. Christ abolishes the old order in that he fulfils and establishes perfectly and for ever the blessings at which it could only aim. His own perfect offering, total obedience to God, includes proleptically the obedience of all who are henceforward to be united to him, and so to come unto God through him. The heart of the argument is in three passages. I give them in a modern translation which is indebted to that of Professor C. F. D. Moule[1] and to the Revised Standard Version.

As the law represents a mere shadow of the blessing that is to be, instead of the real thing, its sacrifices (which are continually offered, year after year) can never make perfect those who draw near. . . . For it is impossible that the blood of bulls and goats should take away sins. Therefore when Christ came into the world, he said, 'sacrifice and offerings thou hast not desired . . . in burnt-offerings and sin-offerings thou hast taken no pleasure. Then said I, Lo I have come (as it is written of me in the roll of the book) to do thy will, O God'. When he said 'Thou hast neither desired nor delighted in sacrifices' (that is, sacrifices offered according to the law) and then added 'Lo, I come to do thy

---

[1] *The Sacrifice of Christ* (Hodder, 1956).

will', he was abolishing the first in order to establish the second. And by that will *we* have been consecrated, through Christ's offering of himself, once for all. Every Temple priest stands daily at his service, offering repeatedly the same sacrifices which can never take away sin. But when Christ had offered, for all time, a single sacrifice for sins, he sat down at the right hand of God. . . .

(Heb. x. 1 – 13.)

The former priests were many in number because they were mortal: death prevented their continuance in office. But he holds his priesthood permanently because he continues for ever. Therefore he is able for all time to save those who draw near to God through him, since he lives for ever to make intercession for them. For it was fitting that we should have such a high priest, holy, blameless, undefiled, separate from sinners, exalted above the heavens. He has no need, like those high priests, to offer sacrifices daily, first for his own sins and then for those of the people. He did this once for all when he offered up himself.

(Heb. vii. 23 f.)

Brethren, since we have confidence to enter the Holy Place by the blood of Jesus, by the new and living way which he opened for us through the Veil (that is, through his flesh), let us draw near with a true heart in absolute assurance of faith.

(Heb. x. 19 f.)

Here, then, the New Testament is witnessing to a sacrifice which is perfect and final. All that was local and temporary, limited and imperfect, is now done away. At the Cross of Jesus there is atonement between God and man which is universal in its import because it is the Lord's doing. He provides the Victim as it were out of his own bosom, for the Victim is his own Son. 'God was in Christ reconciling the world unto himself.' 'Christ our Passover is sacrificed for us; therefore let us keep the feast.' As Ethelbert Stauffer has put it, Good Friday is the Passover-day of universal history. To realize what this means, we should notice the two things it does not mean.

First, there is no separation between the Father and the Son here, as ecclesiastical art has been prone to suggest. This is a truth which the doctrine of the Trinity is meant to conserve. Ecclesiastical art manufacturers have much to answer for: those pictures of the crucified Christ, for example, the tear-filled eyes lifting their pathetic appeal to heaven, and the whole conception of redeeming sacrifice drenched with self-pity and sentimentality.

Like the name *lacrimae Christi* (tears of Christ) given to a Nea-
politan wine, these mass-produced expressions of bad theology
misrepresent what the New Testament is saying throughout,
about Good Friday and Easter Day; about the young prince of
glory doing battle with the powers of darkness, wearing the
crown of thorns as a crown of victory, and reigning over the
world even from the Tree.[1] The New Testament declares that
the saving events of Holy Week are the deed of God; God in the
flesh.

Second, we should notice that there is no separation between
Christ and sinful man here. This is a truth which the doctrine of
the Incarnation is meant to conserve. He who is identified with
the Father through his complete and perfect obedience identifies
himself at the same time, completely and to the uttermost, with
us. It is incontestable that Jesus Christ understood his passion and
death not only as the decisive divine victory over Satan, but also
as a representative sacrificial offering to the Father on behalf of
sinful humanity.

Here, therefore, in one and the same event, is the act both of
God and of man. When Luther wrote 'this Man is God; this God
is Man'[2] he was describing this divine-human act with a daring
which the christological paradox can hardly approve or condemn.
All our words about this Act within the Holy Place will be clumsy
and in some sense erroneous: the daring which is inexcusable is,
nevertheless, inevitable. Did not Hooker warn us that our safest
eloquence concerning him is silence? The christological paradox
is bound up with that other paradox of Law and Gospel with
which we have been specially concerned in this chapter. Ultimately
they are one and the same paradox; Christology and Soteriology
belong together; they are no more separable than are the convex
and concave aspects of one and the same curve. As the systematic
theology of an earlier day would have put it: the Work of Christ

---

[1] Cf. Verse 4 of *Vexilla Regis prodeunt* (Fortunatus):
    Impleta sunt quae concinit
    David fideli carmine,
    Dicens in Nationibus
    Regnabit a ligno Deus.

[2] The Weimar edition of Luther's Works, VI, 512.

is the *ratio cognoscendi* of his person; the Person of Christ is the *ratio essendi* of his work. To put this otherwise: since our redemption must come from God or not at all, it is our experience of judgment and redemption at the Cross which declares this Man to be divine; and since God is in the living and dying of this Man, or there is no God at all, it is his divinity which declares him to be our Redeemer. To put this as it stands in the forefront of the fourth gospel: Behold the Lamb of God which taketh away the sin of the world.

At the Cross the sinless Son of Man was offering himself in perfect obedience as the atoning sacrifice for the sin of man. The Church of his Body is a monument to the fact that it was a representative sacrifice. We participate in his self-offering. The Lord's Supper or Eucharist is the special means of this participation: it is the Christian Passover. Nineteen centuries after his uplifting on Calvary, when his offering for sinners was made once and for all, we the Church of his Body are still drawing near to the same altar of God. We do not come alone. The Lamb of God which taketh away the sin of the world comes with us, since he is one with us for ever. And just as long ago we sinners crucified him,[1] slaying our sacrificial Victim; and just as he took his surrendered and outpoured life (which is our life for ever by our identification with him) through the Veil of his broken flesh into the holy presence of the Father, and atoned for us: so we come now, pleading that eternal sacrifice and participating in it with adoring gratitude (εὐχαριστία). And because Christ-in-his-Church thus offers to the Father the Church-in-himself, 'we offer and present ourselves, our souls and bodies, to be a reasonable holy and living sacrifice'. He makes the offering. He accepts the offering. He receives us. The eternal God with whom we thus have sacred communion, corporate communion, is not only the eternal ground of all being; he is the God and Father of our Lord Jesus Christ. In him deity itself calls saying 'Come': and in him humanity itself makes answer saying 'Lo, I have come'. He answered thus, once and alone, in historic time; but he answers

[1] See p. 145 on 'contemporaneity'.

thus forever and for all mankind διὰ πνεύματος αἰωνίου[1] (through eternal Spirit); that is, in and through the imperishable community of the Spirit, which is the Church.

'Christ our Passover is sacrificed for us: let us keep the feast.'[2]

[1] Heb. ix. 14.
[2] I Cor. v. 7, 8.

CHAPTER IV

THE CROSS AS JUDGMENT AND PENALTY

It is well known that the second line of the greatest hymn in our language has been slightly altered. Watts had first written, 'Where the young prince of glory died', but this yielded later to the somewhat wooden line with which we are familiar.

Watts is often said to have made the change in 1745 when Georgian England was threatened by a Jacobite rising in Scotland, the rebellion of the Young Pretender. The young prince, Charles Edward, was marching south on London, claiming the throne of his ancestors as his by divine right, and quickening in a thousand hearts the old devotion to the house and lineage of the Stuarts. The king was to come to his own again.

> O there were many beating hearts,
> And many a hope and fear,
> And many were the prayers put up
> For the young Chevalier.
> O Charlie is my darling, the young Chevalier.

The rebellion failed. Bonnie Prince Charlie's fair-weather friends fell away and he got no farther than the Midlands. In the end it was only his flight – its details becoming the stuff of romantic legend and song – which saved him from the last humiliation of capture and death. But Watts is said to have hurriedly modified his splendid phrase 'the young prince of glory': the parallel with contemporary politics was too close, too suggestive.

The story is apocryphal, as the best stories often are. 'When I survey the wondrous Cross' was published in 1707 and the second line was altered two years later. And in any case, to Isaac Watts, a sturdy Whig who rejoiced in the collapse of the Young Pretender, the suggestive parallel would have been meaningless and worse.

It was not quite meaningless, however, to a mystique which took the divine right of kings to mean just what it says. For Christ came as a young prince claiming his rightful inheritance. He steadfastly set his face to go to Jerusalem, city of the kings of David's line. He came unto his own. He came as Messiah, the expected Saviour-King for whom all Israel had long been waiting. The crowd on that first Palm Sunday inevitably recalled the thrilling song of the prophet,

> Rejoice greatly, O maiden Zion
> Shout aloud, dear Jerusalem,
> Behold, thy King cometh unto thee.

As we recall those palm-branches and hosannas of the running multitude, the ecstatic, fickle enthusiasm of a city not worthy of such a king, we know that it is our story as well as theirs: it is all men's story; history and faith alike testify to its universal significance. Here is the One who is coming, the expected one (ὁ ἐρχόμενος) who has the supremely authoritative meaning for all human life, and who claims to have it. He bids for nothing less than the fealty of the human race itself, by divine right.

The gospels record the authority which announced itself wherever he was. He spoke with authority, ἐξουσία. But the word in the original Aramaic thus translated into Greek was probably kemōshēl (כְּמָשֵׁל), which means something more; it means that he spoke not merely as teacher but as king. He behaved as a king, in that he exercised a royal freedom even over the divine law given aforetime through Moses. 'Ye have heard that it was said by them of old time . . . but I say unto you.' This means that the royal writ lapses now that the king himself is present and speaking. The authority he claims to exercise is sovereign, redemptive and unique:

Come unto me, all ye that labour and are heavy-laden, and I will give you rest.

The son of man is come to save that which was lost.

The son of man came not to be ministered unto but to minister, and to give his life a ransom for many.

I am come that they might have life, and that they might have it more abundantly.

This is my body which is broken for you.

To this end was I born, and for this cause came I into the world, that I should bear witness unto the truth. Every one that is of the truth heareth my voice.

Art thou the Christ, the Son of the Blessed?
And Jesus said, I am . . . .

Verily I say unto thee, to-day shalt thou be with me in paradise.

The tremendous series of I am's recorded in the fourth gospel,

I am the bread of life; I am the vine; I am the light of the world; I am the door; I am the good shepherd; before Abraham was, I am; I am the resurrection and the life; I am the way, the truth and the life,

could have but one meaning; that here is the sovereign authority of God himself, the *I am that I am*. This language is on the scale of eternity; an uncopyable note sounds in it. If it does not mean that here is One who looks at death and past death conscious that he is therein charged by God with the recovery of the world, language does not mean anything.

I

The Bible is concerned throughout with the Word of God which comes to men in and through the historical event. As we have noticed in an earlier chapter, it is speech with a twofold rhythm of judgment and renewal. Christ not only utters that Word, as did the prophets before him; he embodies it. He *is* the Word of God. God's speech is here translated into the universally intelligible language of a human life, and a human death. Here is God's ultimate self-disclosure to man. 'Last of all, he sent unto them his Son.' In this sending, something absolute and inescapable has come upon our world; first, to judge it: 'for judgment I am come into this world'; second, to redeem it: 'this is a faithful saying and worthy of all acceptation, that Christ Jesus came into the world to save sinners.' The New Testament calls this coming the Kingdom of God.

But men did not believe in or want the kingdom of God after this fashion. Instead of reverencing God's Messiah they reviled and rejected him. He came unto his own but his own received him not. The Roman governor, in whom the rough decencies of imperial justice were at last overborne by shrewd calculation, said to them with contemptuous irony 'Behold your king'; but they cried 'Away with him, crucify him'. Pilate answered 'Shall I crucify your king?' They cried the more, saying 'Let him be crucified'. Whereupon Pilate gave sentence that it should be as they required.

As we stand at the Cross and see what was done there and to whom it was done, are we shocked and indignant? Do we feel a righteous sense of outrage at the cruel cynicism of power politics; at men of religion crying for blood in the name of religion; at disciples betraying their master, or denying him, or running away? Do we pronounce sentence from the judgment seat of our conscious superiority, or even make patronizing allowances for Judas, Caiaphas and the rest on the ground that they lacked the civilizing humaneness of our own enlightened age?

Tediously rhetorical though they are, these questions are worth asking because they remind us that at the Cross alleged degrees of moral achievement are just irrelevant. Quite apart from the awkward difficulty that the era of hydrogen bombs and concentration camps may hardly presume to read a lecture on barbarism to any previous age, here at the Cross no one may judge because all are judged: the events of Holy Week are the final measure of us all, and we are all found wanting.

For the world which put the very prince of life to death is our world. We belong to it, and we cannot disavow the wrongness which has been characteristic of it from the beginning. Indeed, the Cross of Jesus is, in one sense, unspeakably depressing because it shows us ourselves as does no other event in history. It brings to a starkly clear focus the tragic mixture in every one of us. The Cross makes plain, once and for all, that man is evil as well as good, contemptible as well as admirable. He is not only the soaring idealist capable of heroism, self-sacrifice and sainthood; he is also, and at the same time, capable of pride, envy and all uncharitableness; of appalling brutality and degradation. Saying Yes to the divine word which is ever addressed to him, man also says No to it. This is his abiding predicament and tragedy.

We know this at the Cross because there the Kingdom of God is concretely realized; it is fully and finally present. And it is present, first, as judgment. Judgment is an inescapable part of what it means for ever. In the light of holy love which streams from Calvary there is no achievement of man, however fine, however disinterested and heroic, without its accompanying shadow of self-love and pride. The good things about man – the justice of his law, the devotion of his patriotism, the zeal of his religion, the democratic expression of his freedom – are here seen in the presence of God, seen as God sees them. This means that they are seen for what they really are, ever perverted by the deep-seated wrongness, the *permanens infirmitas*,[1] of human nature.

Pilate, for example, was not a particularly bad man. He represented the best government which the ancient world had known, government based on law, the widespread expression of which was the majesty of the Roman peace. Further, he did vindicate the principle of legal justice by repeatedly observing that Jesus was innocent. 'I find no fault in him.' But Pilate illustrates the perennial corruption of justice by political expediency. In his person the Roman empire was not judging Christ, but being judged: and the searching truth is that at the Cross *all* imperialism, whatever its historic form, and however enlightened, disinterested or beneficent it may claim to be, is judged and found wanting.

Again, Caiaphas was not a monster merely because in post-exilic Israel high priesthood had virtually taken the place and function of the old kingship, and therefore enjoyed large executive and judicial powers. He was a patriot whose type abounds; the Grey Eminence of the political scene in all ages; the Grand Inquisitor, cynically devoted to the maintenance of the

---

[1] 'Facta est permanens infirmitas', IV Ezra (II Esdras) iii. 22.

established order, and ready to crush as blasphemy anything which threatens its sacred, privileged stability. Patriotism as the expression of the paramount claims of statesmanship is judged for ever at the Cross of Jesus.

Again, the priests and scribes, the professedly religious leaders of society, were not, as such, evil men: they were merely sure, as religious leaders have been in every generation, that they were consumed with zeal for the Lord, and that their bigoted orthodoxy was ratified in heaven. In fact, however, it slew the prince of life. And the vital point for us is that, in the presence of One whose obedience to the divine goodness is perfect and complete, our fervent righteousness – the very thing on which we rather pride ourselves as showing us at our finest and truest, our religion itself – may turn out to be the 'filthy rags' of self-righteousness which crucifies the Son of God.

Again, the fickle crowd, now eager to crown its king and now to lynch him, was an ordinary crowd, made up of people like ourselves; easily swayed, as we are, by the basest vices of human nature. Good Friday placards for ever the idolatrous claims made for man-in-the-mass and his precious democracy.

Again, the personal friends of Christ who all forsook him and fled were only cowards; which means that none of us dare judge them.

As Jesus moves through the scene these evil things disclose themselves and are judged for what they are. We are made aware that humanity itself is coming up for judgment before him. The story of the Passion has been called 'a masterpiece of dramatic irony'.[1] Ostensibly Jesus is on trial: in reality we are; the world itself is in the dock. 'This is the judgment, that light is come into the world and men love darkness rather than light.' In this searching light of holy love no human life is without an accompanying shadow of idolatrous self-love. The darling self-will of every heart is here made manifest. The sin of man here writes its condemnation on the centre page of history with indelible finality. All men are rebels, so alienated in a far country from him who

[1] C. H. Dodd, *The Bible To-day* (Cambridge, 1943), p. 93.

made them for himself that, when confronted with him there, they seek to destroy him.

And they did destroy him. In one inescapably factual sense the Cross was sheer disaster, the miserable end of the Servant of God in an agony of suffering, loneliness and desolation. But in another sense, which the witness of the New Testament makes equally inescapable, the Cross was no disaster. The apostles and the evangelists nowhere suggest that the Cross was a cruel twist of fortune; that the young prince of glory was here heroically staking all on a final throw – and losing. They see in the dying of the Lord Jesus a necessity lying deep in the eternal counsel of God. Jesus himself knew that his death would be due not merely to the guilty human passions which would bring it about, but to 'the determinate counsel and foreknowledge of God'.[1] For it is the huge paradox, the outrageous originality of the gospel of our redemption, that the divine judgment on man's whole evil situation falls upon the divine judge. He, the innocent One, bears in his own body and being those penal consequences of man's ill-doing and guilt which are his own judgment upon sin. Judgment and penalty are one and the same fact in Christ crucified.

II

The New Testament clue to this paradox is provided by the Old Testament, the four songs in the second part of the book of Isaiah which describe the Suffering Servant of God, his character and calling, his redemptive suffering and death. The clue is first disclosed by Jesus himself, who sees in the last and greatest of these songs a prophetic description of his own calling and destiny. The words of Isaiah liii became the most authoritative and precious of the ancient 'testimonies' to Christ treasured by the early Church, not only because they had been thus used in prophetic vision, but also because they had filled the vision of the Redeemer himself, entering his gospel, shaping his redeeming way among men, and issuing in his Cross. Here is the Song:[2]

---

[1] Acts ii. 23.

[2] The translation is that of the Revised Standard Version (Nelson, 1952).

3. He was despised and rejected by men;
    a man of sorrows and acquainted with grief;
And as one from whom men hide their faces
    he was despised, and we esteemed him not.

4. Surely he has borne our griefs
    and carried our sorrows;
Yet we esteemed him stricken,
    smitten by God, and afflicted.

5. But he was wounded for our transgressions,
    he was bruised for our iniquities;
Upon him was the chastisement that made us whole,
    and with his stripes we are healed.

6. All we like sheep have gone astray;
    we have turned everyone to his own way;
And the Lord has laid on him
    the iniquity of us all.

7. He was oppressed, and he was afflicted,
    yet he opened not his mouth;
Like a lamb that is led to the slaughter,
    and like a sheep that before its shearers is dumb,
So he opened not his mouth.

8. By oppression and judgment he was taken away;
    and as for his generation, who considered
That he was cut off out of the land of the living,
    stricken for the transgression of my people?

9. And they made his grave with the wicked
    and with a rich man in his death,
Although he had done no violence,
    and there was no deceit in his mouth.

10. Yet it was the will of the Lord to bruise him;
    he has put him to grief;
When he makes himself an offering for sin,
    he shall see his offspring, he shall prolong his days;
The will of the Lord shall prosper in his hand;

11. He shall see the fruit of the travail of his soul
    and be satisfied;
By his knowledge shall the righteous one, my servant,
    make many to be accounted righteous;
And he shall bear their iniquities.

12. Therefore I will divide him a portion with the great,
   and he shall divide the spoil with the strong;
   Because he poured out his soul to death,
   and was numbered with the transgressors;
   Yet he bore the sin of many,
   and made intercession for the transgressors.

This great song presents some notorious difficulties. Its role in the life of the Church has been so momentous that we want to know what its author meant in detail and as a whole; but we do not know with certainty. There are textual obscurities: and the Septuagint version differs materially from the Hebrew text, notably in the crucial fourth verse. There is the famous problem of the Servant's identity: was the unknown prophet of the Babylonian exile writing here about Israel as a corporate personality (as seems most probable), or about the faithful Remnant; or about some contemporary or future individual leader?

Our immediate concern, however, is with the final issue to which these preliminary considerations lead, the religious and theological meaning of the Servant's sufferings and death. This meaning seems to be twofold. The song makes use of *two* of those three biblical metaphors which have given rise to the three classic types of atonement theology within the Christian Church. To recall what we have already noticed in previous chapters, they are the metaphors of victory, sacrifice and penalty. Taken from the battlefield, the altar and the law-court they are, respectively, redemptive, expiatory and penal in content; by dying, Christ rescues us from Satan, offers the perfect sacrifice and bears the penalty of our sin.

The song, then, brings together and blends two of these metaphors: sacrifice and penalty. Admittedly it alludes to the sacrificial system only once, in its tenth verse; but the allusion is clear and unmistakable; the Servant's death is represented as an *asham* (אָשָׁם) or guilt-offering. On the other hand the song makes twelve distinct and explicit statements that the Servant suffers the *penalty* of other men's sins: not only vicarious suffering but penal substitution is the plain meaning of its fourth, fifth and sixth verses. These may not be precise statements of Western forensic ideas, but they are clearly concerned with penalty, inflicted through various forms of punishment which the Servant endured on other men's behalf and in their stead, because the Lord so ordained. This legal or law-court metaphor of atonement may be stated positively or negatively: either as penalty which the Redeemer takes upon himself, or as acquittal which sets the prisoner free. But in either way of stating it the connotation is substitutionary:

> In my place condemned he stood;
> Sealed my pardon with his blood.

To put this in its most offensive and difficult form, the Christian religion has thought of the Christ not only as Victor and as Victim, but also as 'Criminal'. The incarnate, yet sinless, One was 'made sin' on our behalf. He was so identified with the guilty sinners whom he was to deliver and save that he was actually reckoned as one of them and treated accordingly. And whatever may be thought of later theological statements of this identification, it had its historic origin and basis in Christ's own recognition and acceptance of it. He quoted the twelfth verse of this very song and applied it explicitly to himself. 'One text of scripture is bound to come true for me, "he was counted among the criminals": my life is coming to an end.'[1] From the beginning, and sometimes with a crudity and daring which have hardly helped its evangelical purpose, the Church has used this treatment of Christ as criminal to expound the gospel of redeeming grace, and to say *how* God 'justifies the ungodly'.[2] 'Himself bare our sins in his own body on the tree.'[3] 'Christ has redeemed us from the curse of the law, having become a curse for us.'[4] Only against this background may we understand Luther's highly extravagant rhetoric which describes Christ as 'the greatest of all sinners' because 'he assumed in his body the sins we had committed, to make satisfaction for them by his own blood'. This is an extreme expression of that theology of penal substitution which has

---

[1] Luke xxii. 37; T. W. Manson's translation.
[2] Rom. iv. 5.
[3] I Pet. ii. 24.
[4] Gal. iii. 13.

characterized and even dominated the piety and worship, the liturgies and formal systems of Western Christendom, Catholic and Protestant.

But even when it is not stated extravagantly, penal substitution is a very difficult concept because it is morally offensive. Are there any considerations which mitigate the offence and so make this language of the law-court more 'worthy of acceptation'? If so they must come from the New Testament itself.

We notice first that this concept occurs rarely in the New Testament. Whereas the imagery of Christ as Victor is varied and abundant in gospels and epistles, and whereas there is weighty, albeit less frequent, evidence for the sacrificial imagery of Christ as Victim, there is relatively little evidence to support the concept of penal substitution as later developed. What evidence there is occurs mainly in St Paul; and is virtually limited to the two passages already cited, Galatians iii. 13 and II Corinthians v. 21.

We should notice in the second place that each of these two passages stops short of the unflinching logic of penal substitution. Galatians iii. 13 reads:

Christ redeemed us from the curse of the law, having been made a curse for us (γενόμενος ὑπὲρ ἡμῶν κατάρα). For it is written, Cursed be everyone who hangs on a tree (ἐπικατάρατος πᾶς ὁ κρεμάμενος ἐπὶ ξύλου).

Here the ancient idea of the curse is applied to the death of Christ, the 'proof-text' being Deuteronomy xxi. 22 – 3, which reads:

If a man has committed a crime punishable by death, and he is put to death, and you hang him on a tree, his body shall not remain all night upon the tree, but you shall bury him the same day; for a hanged man is accursed by God (ὑπὸ τοῦ θεοῦ: LXX). You shall not defile your land which the Lord your God gives you for an inheritance.

The vital consideration here is that this passage about the Curse does not occur in the calmer and fuller statement of the same argument in Romans. There, at the same point in a parallel argument, St Paul omits the appeal to the ancient ruling that a criminal is, as such, accursed. But even in the impassioned argument of Galatians where he does make this appeal, he omits the words 'by God' after 'accursed': he does not use the logic of the Deuteronomic law to say that Christ crucified was *maledictus dei*, as Luther was to do. Indeed, he does not actually say that Christ was accursed; he uses instead the strange expression (which anticipates our second passage, II Cor. v. 21) that Christ *became* or *was made* a curse. In brief, at more than one point, St Paul stops short of the logic of his proof-text; and in his later amplification of the same argument in a calmer mood he drops the proof-text altogether. It is not regulative for his thought as a whole. Like the passage which follows immediately in Galatians iv. 1ff. (and which is introduced with the apologetic, deprecatory words, κατὰ ἄνθρωπον λέγω) it is a rabbinical *argumentum ad hominem*. It is certainly not the Pauline gospel.

The other passage is II Cor. v. 21 which reads: 'For our sake he (God) made him to be sin who knew no sin, so that in him we might become the righteousness of God.' Here that strange expression 'made a curse' is matched by the equally strange 'made sin' about which, as J. K. Mozley put it,[1] we can safely say that, whatever it does mean, it does not mean 'was made a sinner'. St Paul neither says nor means that Christ was 'made guilt' for us, as though the Father treated his sinless Son as a sinner in order that he might not treat sinners as such. We may not dot the *i* and cross the *t* of a single phrase in this way, since there is little if any comparable evidence from St Paul's thought to support and justify it.

There is a further consideration. The New Testament as a whole gives little or no supporting evidence for the contention that these two isolated Pauline passages justify an explicitly vicarious or substitutionary interpretation of the Cross. Here the use which the early Church made of the song is illuminating. We have already noticed that the substitutionary aspect of the Servant's suffering and death, which is so pronounced in the Hebrew text of Isaiah liii, is a good deal less apparent in the Septuagint version. The early Church was plainly aware of this; for, to quote Professor G. W. H. Lampe,[2] 'Although the Servant poems are freely employed in the primitive Church to prove that death was not

---

[1] *The Doctrine of the Atonement* (Duckworth, 1927), p. 78.

[2] *Reconciliation in Christ* (Longmans, 1956), p. 42.

incompatible with Messiahship and that the Son of God took the form of a slave; and although it is most probable that these passages were understood by Jesus himself as pointing to the character of his own mission, the particular texts which, at least as we read the Hebrew version, seem to favour a "substitutionary" interpretation of his death as a punishment inflicted on him by God in place of sinners, or as a satisfaction made to God's justice, *are not in fact quoted*' (my italics). It seems legitimate to argue, therefore, that though the three classic metaphors of atonement theology are all found in the New Testament, its main witness is to Christ as Victor and as Victim; and that though the juridical concept of vicarious penalty is also found in the statements that he was 'made sin', and 'made a curse', and that he 'bore our sins in his own body on the tree', it is hardly justifiable to build a precise dogmatic scheme on so slender and uncertain a foundation.

The enduring importance of this evidence lies in what it is saying about the uniqueness, the revolutionary newness of Christ's death. To realize this we have to recall a theme of our previous chapter for a moment, the meaning of sacrifice in the Old Testament period.

We saw that sacrifice meant the death of an animal victim whereby its life was released and offered to God at the altar. This death was pure and sacred; it had none of the impure and defiling associations of the gallows, such as are described in Deuteronomy xxi. 23. Indeed, two kinds of death are distinguished in the Old Testament; the surrendering of life falls into one or other of two opposed categories. On the one hand, there is the holy death of the sacrificial victim, devoted entirely to God, and therefore entirely consumed (by fire or other means), lest it should come to corruption. On the other hand, there is the unholy penal death of the criminal, who is 'accursed' and as such cut off from God; its outcome is the corruption of the grave. The subject of the first kind of death is an animal, unblemished, innocent and sacred: as victim it is never contaminated with the sin of him who offers it. The subject of the second kind of death is man, sinful, unholy, and the bearer of sin's penalty in the doom of death. This categorical difference explains why sin-bearing and sacrifice are mutually exclusive in the Old Testament. Throughout its whole period they normally stand over against one another, presenting a contrast. On the annual Day of Atonement it is solemnly and dramatically emphasized.

Against this background of contrast and mutual exclusion the song in Isaiah liii stands out as witnessing to something new. Here the notions of sin-bearing and sacrifice cease to be contrasted; they are combined. The Servant is described *both* as sin-bearer and as sacrifice. The fourth and the following verses are neither separated from nor contrasted with the tenth verse. The song is an unbroken sequence throughout. The Servant's redeeming death is the fact uniting and virtually identifying categories hitherto different and distinct.

This, however, is still idea rather than fact. Even if it was Israel in exile, or the faithful Remnant of Israel, whom the prophet saw to be the Suffering Servant of the Lord, his vision had not yet been concretely realized as historic fact. As we must notice in the next chapter,[1] the nation could not be the bearer of the divine revelation in that perfect and final sense. That could happen only in a personal human life. Christianity claims that it did happen, once for all, in Christ crucified.

It is hardly surprising, then, that the primitive Church looked back to this song as *the* proof-text of the wonderfully new fact which had brought it into being. In the New Testament both sin-bearing and sacrifice are descriptions of one and the same fact because Christ himself was the new fact, the new and final revelation here. The divine love in Christ was willing to share the unlovely death of the criminal, which is sin's penalty. Thus the unholy and common death which is the due fate of all men was transformed at the Cross into the holy and unique death of perfect sacrifice. By dying as he did Jesus 'changed penalty into sacrifice, and shame into glory; and by his risen life enables his faithful followers to do the same'.[2]

---

[1] See p. 92 below.
[2] O. C. Quick, *The Gospel of the New World* (Nisbet, 1944), p. 101.

III

We have already noticed that theories of atonement are efforts to state in words or images the paradox of forgiveness in judgment, the divine mercy in the divine wrath. They are our stammering recognition that the divine mercy cannot affect its holy purpose unless the seriousness of sin is fully disclosed and known. Critics of Anselm's *Cur Deus Homo* have always to meet the scrutiny of its most famous sentence: *nondum considerasti quanti ponderis sit peccatum* (thou hast not yet considered how great is the weight of sin). Forgiveness is neither intelligible nor credible unless justice is vindicated and guilt confirmed.[1] The sentimental interpretation of the divine love is a lie. The consciousness of guilt cannot be overcome by the facile formula that because God is love man is forgiven. There can be no simple abrogation of the wrath of God by the mercy of God. As Tillich observes somewhere, 'the mercy of God represents the ultimate freedom of God above his own law, not the repudiation of that law'. God vindicates his own law by accepting and bearing its penalty in his own heart.

This is why the problem of salvation with which we have been concerned all along has the problem of atonement at its heart. How does the moral fact of our estrangement from the Holy One become the religious fact of our acceptance by him and our reconciliation to him? The alienation which distorts all the relationships of our existence, but from which God redeems us by participating therein to the uttermost – how are we to picture this? How does this redemptive participation 'work'?

Since God is holy the only true satisfaction which the sinner can make is obedience: a return to the holiness against which he has been in rebellion. Will not repentance, coupled with amendment of life, be the one thing needful, then; and the only thing possible?

Repentance is certainly a vital condition of reconciliation: atonement which left it out would be a mockery. Yet even

[1] See p. 46 above.

repentance does not get us to the real problem, the ultimate issue – which is our guilt. Aware of our guilt to the depth of our being, we know that no easy assertion of God's love towards us would be able to deal effectively with this, our real predicament. For our past is there: rivers of tears cannot wash it away. The evil that I have done, and the evil that I have set afloat in lives now far beyond my reach or control, is objective fact for ever. My very knowledge that God cannot condone it is the meaning and measure of guilt. Is it possible, or even conceivable, that – in spite of all this, and of the despair which is its correlative – God should restore us sinners to fellowship with himself, vindicating in the very manifestation of that restoration the holiness which we have flouted? Is it abstractly possible that there might be a holiness which could atone to holiness: that human history might be used as the divine instrument for manifesting the uttermost of redeeming love in terms of the uttermost of holy obedience?

The gospel is what it is, good news, because it is the historic actuality of this abstract possibility. It manifests an obedience so complete and perfect as to meet the divine holiness on the scale of human guilt: winning the victory over evil; making the perfect sacrifice; dying the human death; and giving us part and lot for ever in this threefold action and passion.

Christ crucified accepts the judgment which holiness must ever pass upon man's sin. He confesses that judgment to be holy from amid the deepest experience of it; the experience not of a spectator but of a participant. His perfect obedience is not adequately described as a unique and wonderful harmony between his will and the will of the Father. It was the willing acceptance, on our behalf, of that judgment which our sin had entailed; it was the confession, on our behalf, in a tremendous act, that the judgment of God is just and holy.

The inadequacy of all such exposition is obvious. Explanatory words such as 'acceptance' and 'confession' fail us, since here is something which cannot be explained. 'To explain' means 'to put into a class'. But this is unique; it belongs to no class; it is a particular which is its own universal. It involves the ultimate mystery of christology. Analogies furnished from human experience do not resolve that mystery: they serve only to state and leave it as such. Dr Ryder Smith[1] has recorded Forsyth's story of Schamyl, the chief of the fierce heroes of the Caucasus in their long struggle against the Russians. At one time some unknown traitor was giving away the secrets of Schamyl's little band, and he issued an order that the next person found communicating with the enemy in any way should be scourged. Presently there was an astounding solution to the mystery: the culprit was discovered, and it was Schamyl's mother. For two days he disappeared within his tent. Then he emerged, worn out with his misery and shame. He bade his men strip him and bind him to the stake, and to scourge him, instead of his mother, with the knout.

That there is some analogy between this moving story of vicarious penalty and Calvary is obvious; but the limitation and ultimate irrelevance of such analogy is also obvious. For if there be any truth in the christological paradox that God was in Christ, we cannot hope to hold together in our minds 'the objectivity of Christ's work *towards* God and its subjectivity in God'.[2] That would involve the absurdity that we could embrace the consciousness of God within our own consciousness.

The story of Schamyl illustrates the almost unendurable tension between conflicting loyalties on the human level. The story of Gethsemane and Calvary is, so to speak, on the two levels of the divine and the human, since as Son of God the Redeemer is at one with the Father, and as Son of Man he is at one with sinners whom he is not ashamed to call his brethren. The grace of our Lord Jesus Christ, which identified him with the holy love of God, also identified him with sinners completely and to the uttermost; he felt the reality and weight of sin as though it had been his own; he carried vicariously the burden of human guilt on the heart of his divine humanity; and as he utters the Cry of

---

[1] C. Ryder Smith, *The Bible Doctrine of Salvation* (Epworth, 1946), p. 9.

[2] H. Wheeler Robinson in *The Christian Faith*, ed. W. R. Matthews (London, 1936), p. 222.

Dereliction (Mark xv. 34) we see him stagger under its weight. He makes satisfaction to the father; but since there can be no ultimate or even temporary separation between the Father and the Son,[1] his satisfaction is, *ineffabili modo*, the Father's self-satisfaction. (If this last sentence should prove to be some form of modalist or patripassian heresy, I withdraw it, since heresy is far from my wish or intention, even though I cannot help remembering Fairbairn's remark that patripassianism is only half a heresy. My intention is not to depart from the orthdox wisdom of the centuries, but to avoid the proven dangers of 'transactional' theology as carefully as I should wish to avoid those of a crypto-monophysitism. This is a note for theologians, and for anyone else who, like me, tries to take dogma seriously and to learn from it.) The Cross is the place where sinful men come nearest to understanding what sin must mean to the holy love of God. The Man called Christ is the only man in history who has seen sin for what it really is, seen it (that is) as God sees it, and said Amen to the penal judgment of holiness upon it. Only Christ, in the sinless perfection of his obedience, could truly feel the holiness of God in its judgment of sin. He alone, therefore, could confess and honour it. No son of Adam could do this because none could repent with *due* and *perfect* repentance. Christ alone could know the agony of being 'forsaken' by God, since he alone is indissociably one with him. The Cry of Dereliction is not really intelligible therefore, save from the heart of the incarnate Redeemer, the Word made flesh. It reveals him as indissolubly one with the very Father who cannot look on sin 'save to abhor and curse it even when his Son is beneath it' (P. T. Forsyth). God redeems at this tremendous cost; and this is the meaning of that metaphor of penalty which has been continuously blended with the different yet cognate metaphors of victory and sacrifice, in the Christian gospel of redemption.

[1] See p. 57 above.

NOTE

As an appendix to the foregoing chapters a scheme of contrasts is set out below. It attempts to differentiate those Eastern and Western types of Christianity which became distinctive during the first five centuries. Its generalizations lose what validity they have as soon as they are unduly pressed.

EAST	WEST
1 Greek	1 Latin
2 Its genius is speculative	2 Its genius is practical
3 Its temper is philosophical and individualistic	3 Its temper is legalistic and authoritarian
4 Emphasis on doctrine	4 Emphasis on polity
5 To Origen Christianity was a system of divine truth, able to win for itself the reason and conscience of every man	5 To Cyprian Christianity was a divine polity imposed by authority
6 Thought is all-important	6 Law is all-important
7 The arch-foe is Heresy	7 The arch-foe is Schism
8 In the Greek type of piety the central theme is Incarnation: the recreation of Man in God's Image	8 In the Latin type of piety the central theme is Atonement: the tremendous cost of God's saving Grace
9 Origen's presuppositions are ultimately ontological	9 Augustine's presuppositions are ultimately anthropological
10 The Greeks are mainly concerned with the relation of φθορά to ἀφθαρσία	10 The Latins are mainly concerned with the relation of *peccatum* to *salus*
11 The metaphors characteristic of Greek soteriology are sacramental and realistic: ἀνακεφαλαίωσις and θεοποίησις	11 The metaphors characteristic of Latin soteriology are sacrificial and forensic: *hostia* and *satisfactio*
12 Christ is God, assuming human nature, to deify humanity	12 Christ is Man, offering atoning sacrifice to God, qualified thereto by his divine nature
13 Victor	13 Victim
14 Incarnation as the rationale of Atonement	14 Atonement as the rationale of Incarnation
15 Greek Christology: Incarnate God	15 Latin Christology: Divine Man
16 Αὐτὸς ἐνηνθρώπησεν ἵνα ἡμεῖς θεοποιηθῶμεν (Irenaeus and Athanasius)	16 'Homo dominicus'. 'In quantum Homo in tantum Mediator' (Augustine)
17 Antioch: Alexandria: Constantinople	17 Carthage: Rome
18 ὀρθοδοξία	18 *Tu es Petrus . . .*

CHAPTER V

THE OFFENCE OF PARTICULARITY

'What a narrow-minded man you are, to suppose that your Jesus is alone important, all other great ones counting for nothing. There are many great men, many seers, many leaders.'[1] Goethe wrote thus in 1780 to his friend Lavater, whose epic poem *Jesus Messias* had just appeared. The intimacy of several years was broken by this sudden attack, which included charges of hypocrisy and superstition.

The charge of hypocrisy was a denial that Lavater was, in fact, the champion of orthodoxy which he seemed and claimed to be. Opposed though he was to the aridities of rationalism, he had, as Goethe shrewdly perceived, a mystic's indifference to the inexpugnable historical element in the Christian revelation.

The charge of superstition was more surprising, coming as it did from Goethe. It was the stock weapon employed by the Encyclopaedists and others in that age of reason to attack the very idea of a unique divine revelation in the fulness of time. In the name of Enlightenment (*Aufklärung*) they reduced Christianity to its deistic 'essentials' and then argued that it was 'not mysterious' and 'as old as Creation'. Goethe had little sympathy with mere iconoclasm of this kind; he was the great Romantic for whom the green and golden tree of life made all rationalizing theory grey by comparison.[2] Yet his splenetic attack on Lavater's sentimentalities betrayed his kinship with the prevailing temper of his age. That one of his intimates should even seem to assert the uniqueness of the Word made flesh was offensively narrow-minded.

[1] 'Du engherziger Mensch daß du meinst nur dein Jesus gelte etwas, alle andern Großen gelten nichts. Es gibt so viele großen Menschen, viele Weise, viele Führer.'

[2] 'Grau, teurer Freund, ist alle Theorie
Und grün des Lebens goldner Baum.' *Faust*, Part I.

I

That there is a real difficulty here is obvious. It was not peculiar to the eighteenth century. Ever since astronomy made the old geocentric conception of the universe impossible, the witness of the New Testament to the cosmic uniqueness of God's deed in Christ has been a stumbling-block to the Western intellect. Gerhard Kittel's now classic phrase for it – '*das Ärgernis der Einmaligkeit*' (the scandal of particularity) – may indicate that it is still the most formidable difficulty which modern Christian apologetic has to tackle. The biblical view of history seems too narrow. Have not other nations besides ancient Israel received distinctive revelations of religious truth? And, in any case, is not the relativity inherent in the revelation made to any particular generation, or through particular persons, an insuperable obstacle to claims to absoluteness made on its behalf? This is the issue which Troeltsch set out in all its bearings in *Die Absolutheit des Christentums und die Religionsgeschichte* (1902), and which the comparative study of religions sharpens.

For example, Buddhism, Christianity and Islam are great and long-established world-religions. Each has millions of adherents and is, on this ground alone, too important to be ignored. Further, each makes a universal claim and bids for the allegiance of mankind, irrespective of divisions of race or nationality, since each has the same three characteristics.

First, each professes to rest on a *revelation*, a self-disclosure of the eternal order within the visible, familiar, temporal order. Second, for each this revelation is *given*, in some sense; it was mediated through a special, individual and unrepeatable situation; it was not something excogitated, as laws of logic or mathematics are, by a process of philosophical reflection. (Buddhism is hardly an exception here, for though it originated with the reflections of the prince Gautama Siddartha beneath the bodhi tree, it is what it is because it developed all the institutional concreteness of a revealed religion. Whitehead's aphorism that Christianity is a religion looking for a metaphysic, whereas Buddhism

G
81

is a metaphysic looking for a religion, does not invalidate their formal parallelism as world religions: seen as a whole, each is a missionary faith enunciating absolute truth received by revelation in past time.) Third, for each the given revelation is the final truth about human existence; it is not provisional and therefore subject to replacement by something more adequate in the course of time; it is 'once for all'.

These facts raise three major difficulties. The first is logical: distinctive and different revelations, each claiming to be divinely given and therefore final, are incompatible; they cancel one another out. The second is historical: each of these historical religions has had to discriminate between permanent and passing elements in its revelation: between its unchanging, essential substance and certain accidental features which permit and require restatement, as the intellectual climate of successive generations changes. The third is philosophical: there is an inescapable critical question for thought; namely, whether any revelation rooted in history can have a final, unchanging and therefore unprogressive character (which is what the claim to finality implies), even when its accidental elements have been 'demythologized' or otherwise quietly eliminated.[1]

The question, then, which that *saeculum rationalisticum*, the eighteenth century, was asking was whether there must not be ideally, and whether there should not be actually one universal religion and only one; confined rigidly (as Kant put it) 'within the bounds of pure reason': a natural theology purged of all alleged supernatural particularities; the religion, in brief, of all sensible men.

We need not call upon Freud or modern depth-psychology to expose the naïveté here, since St Augustine and Luther, Montaigne and Pascal, Bunyan and the Wesleys had already done it, probing what St Augustine had called the depths of the human heart (*abyssus humanae conscientiae*), and telling the truth about its weakness. And history might have reminded the age of the Augustans that few men are moved much, and none solely, by

[1] Cf. A. E. Taylor, *The Faith of a Moralist* (Macmillan, 1931), II, 43 – 4.

rational considerations. We do not tame one of the master passions of mankind by putting it into the strait-waistcoat of rationalism. But, on the other hand, the eighteenth century was more right than wrong in its urbane refusal to make religion synonymous with bigotry. And here I turn to Professor J. B. Mayor's comment on James i. 19 – 20:[1]

He is speaking of the way in which men should receive the Word. 'They should be quick to hear, slow to speak, slow to wrath, seeing that the wrath of man does not work the righteousness of God; therefore they are to receive with meekness the word of salvation.' On a first reading we might be inclined to ask, Who ever supposed that man's wrath could work God's righteousness? Why should St James have given utterance to a truism like this? But the history of religion proves that there is no more common delusion than this – that the best evidence a man can give of his own orthodoxy is his bitterness towards the heterodoxy of others. The monarch's private vices were atoned for by his unsparing persecution of his heretical subjects; to join a crusade against the infidel was regarded as a passport to heaven; to burn a Protestant was an Act of Faith. The *odium theologicum* has passed into a proverb.

Mayor goes on to analyse the ways in which religion stimulates hope and fear and the human longing for assurance. The fact that this assurance

is liable to be shaken by the discovery that others do not acknowledge the same authority is one main cause of the hatred of heresy, as tending to undermine a man's own faith and destroy his own security. Then this very hatred – itself, as we have seen, the offspring of doubt and fear – becomes identified in our thoughts with righteous indignation against sin; and the more fiercely it rages, the stronger is the conviction in the mind of the persecutor, that he is the Jehu appointed to carry out the Divine vengeance against the sinner, and that Paradise is secure to the champion of the truth. Something of the same kind may be observed wherever party spirit (ἐριθία) runs high; it is so easy, so comforting, to be a good hater, to take for granted that one's own side has a monopoly of intellect and virtue, to accept the party watchword and join in shouting the party war-cry; so arduous and so humbling to divest oneself of prejudice, to seek the truth for its own sake, to acknowledge the evil in ourselves, and see the good in those who differ from us.

Evidently we have 'to keep the mean between two extremes, of too much stiffness . . . and too much easiness' even when confessing with angels and archangels and with all the company of heaven that Particular which is its own Universal, the redemption of the world by our Lord Jesus Christ.

[1] *The Epistle of St James* (Macmillan, 1892), pp. 195 – 6.

II

There is something indecent about poking at the deepest thing by which men live with the coarse finger of critical scrutiny, but we should scrutinize this element of particularity in the Hebraic-Christian revelation if only because it is a stumbling-block and foolishness to many a modern man, just as it was to many contemporaries of St Paul.

The particularity is a stumbling-block not so much because of what it asserts, but because of what it omits and virtually excludes. It asserts the redemptive uniqueness of certain specific historical events; the absolute significance of a particular historical process which became dynamic in Palestine some three thousand years ago; and of a particular Person who was its fulfilment and final meaning in 'the fulness of time'. 'Once for all at the consummation of the ages he was manifested' (Heb. ix. 26). 'No man cometh to the Father but by me' (John xiv. 6).

It is a notorious difficulty that vast sequences of human experience across the continents and the centuries seem to be ignored or even repudiated in this sublime climax. No problem, not even that of christology (with which, of course, it is bound up), vexes the modern Christian mind with so nagging a persistence as this does. 'You only have I known of all the families of the earth' (Amos iii. 2). If these words, spoken on behalf of God, had come to the notice of, say, Xenophanes of Colophon two centuries later, what would he have thought of them? Their meaning, *prima facie*, seems to be that the God of the whole earth has no interest in the Greeks; and is therefore not far removed from a tribal deity after all. If it does not commit us to this absurdity, is it substantially different, *mutatis mutandis*, from what John Milton was to write two thousand years later about 'God' Englishmen'? Just because the partisan, exclusive temper, deplored as a shameful human failing by the great scholar quoted above, pervades man's history even at its highest levels, is it no baffling to find it where we might have expected it to be completely transcended? To China, which as the oldest of civili nations has an unbroken cultural tradition of over four thousand years, the rest of mankind were Outer Barbarians, inherently inferior to the sons of Han: we smile at this cool assumption much as we do at Sir Fopling Flutter in the Restoration play who pronounces that 'beyond Hyde Park all is desert'. And we might smile at Kipling's

> Such boastings as the Gentiles use
> Or lesser breeds without the Law,

were it not that his very metaphor is Hebraic, and would be unintelligible apart from the sacred scriptures of the 'chosen people'.

Granted that human activities, remembered and interpreted as historical events, do give actuality in time to the judging and redeeming purpose of God, must their selection be exclusively limited to the Hebraic-Christian tradition? Why may not the events of Israel's history be treated as examples, admittedly striking and effective, but no more than examples, of a general and universal principle of revelation? Why should not all events of history be patient, at least, of an equally significant interpretation by discerning religious faith? Is Israel the only nation from China to Peru who may praise the Lord of history for his mighty acts?

The Christian religion is, as we must notice in the next section, universal in its range and meaning; but it is so only against the background of this offensive particularity which it admits and accentuates. It is not content to declare that though all historic events, being unique and unrepeatable, may be vehicles of creative revelation, here is one which is significant and transforming in the highest *degree*. It declares that here is something unique in *kind*: 'the unique and absolute entrance of the kingdom of God into human experience. *The Word was made flesh*. No more absolute relation of God to history than that can be conceived.'[1]

The New Testament witness comes from men whose main concern is not with general truths, religious and moral. Their purpose is not even, as in legends of the Buddha, to illustrate 'noble truths' about suffering and its ultimate resolution, with

[1] C. H. Dodd, *The Apostolic Preaching* (Hodder, 1936), p. 232.

examples drawn from the life of a Master. Their witness is to an unprecedented, unrepeatable event which took place at one point in time, and so changed, once for all, the face of history and the relationship between time and eternity. This 'onceness', 'once-for-allness', is of the essence of the New Testament witness: it is likened by the epistle to the Hebrews to the unique significance which death has for the destiny of the individual man. 'For just as it is appointed for man to die once, and after that comes judgment; so Christ was offered once to bear the sins of many' (ix. 27). In this and in previous verses (ix. 12, 26) the word ἅπαξ (once) is used again and again, as it is in I Peter iii. 18 and in Romans vi. 10. 'Christ suffered once for our sins.' 'The death he died he died for sin, once for all.'

The gospel (which has the particularity of a story rather than the generality of a philosophy) begins with this unique, world-transforming event. The kingdom of God is here (Mark i. 15) in that Jesus sees, on rising from the water of baptism, 'the heavens split open' (σχιζομένους τοὺς οὐρανούς, Mark i. 10). The words belong to ancient cosmology, according to which the solid firma-ment of heaven, like an inverted bowl, held up the cosmic water and the stars, above the level earth. Karl Heim's exegetical comment is worth quoting because it makes no attempt to soft-pedal the *Einmaligkeit* to which the New Testament bears unambiguous witness.

The long-shut sphere of the divine transcendence is opened: the silence of God, which had lain like a leaden sky over the centuries since the silence of the law of the prophets, has come to an end. The time is now fulfilled and the hour is striking. This event is described by the New Testament as a sheer gift for which man can never be sufficiently grateful (χάρις, χαρισθῆναι); or as σωτηρία, the saving of shipwrecked humanity which would otherwise drown in the abyss.

As theologian and mathematician, aware that modern Christian apologetic has to use the thought-world of modern physics, Heim might have illustrated the opened heavens of Mark i. 10

---

[1] *Jesus der Herr* (Berlin, 1935), p. 166.

[2] Cf. *Glaube und Denken: Grundlegung einer christlichen Lebensanschauung* (Berlin, 1934, pp. 57 – 89.

from the modern astronomical observatory, with a section of the over-arching dome rolled back and stellar galaxies of unimaginable vastness revealing their ultimate mystery to a speck of wayside dust – our little corner of the insignificant solar system. The scandal of particularity.

III

The Christian apologist makes a fourfold answer to the familiar and formidable difficulty which has been outlined in the two previous sections of this chapter.

In the first place, particularity (in the sense already discussed) seems to be unavoidable, by modern as well as by ancient man, by astro-physicist as well as by Christian theologian. It is an inalienable structure of our experience. So far from representing a perversely narrowed outlook it is the way we get at our universals. The ultimate becomes actual only through the concrete, the universal only through the particular. *Universalia in rebus.*

It would not be extravagant to say that the universally human which declares itself in history is first manifest in a special place and in a particular group. The dramatic illustrations of this fact are obvious and accepted. There is what G. M. Trevelyan called a 'mystical element' in all great revolutions, when a nation or class, long sunk – it may be – in servitude or mediocrity, suddenly flashes out in all the splendour of human energy. The wind bloweth where it listeth. There is a tide in the affairs of men. We cannot 'account for' the age of Pericles, the age of Elizabeth, or (*pace* Marxist determinism) the creative energies of modern Russia, any more than we can account for and so 'explain' Plato, Shakespeare or Mozart. 'Whatever it may be in speculation,' wrote Butler, 'freedom is a fact.' And particularity is its correlative. In the light of our modern discoveries and rediscoveries about ourselves this means that an irreducible datum of particularity has to be accepted by sociologist or medical psychologist at the end of all their 'nomothetic' generalizations about man in terms of his biological relatedness, the unconscious drives of the mass-psyche, and the pre-rational levels or sub-rational deeps of

his life as *animal symbolicum*.[1] Something wayward and incal-
culable may at any time say No to those 'laws' which are valuable
statistical averages throwing light on what happens in individuals
and societies, and making prediction feasible and valid. This
'idiographic'[2] element may not be discounted as merely a provisional confession of ignorance pending the arrival of the final
determinist formula: the particular and the contingent will still
be at hand to call its bluff.

Natural science, still popularly supposed to be exclusively
nomothetic, seems demonstrably so as astronomy, the science of
the stars:

> ... rank on rank
> The army of unalterable Law.[3]

But in his famous paragraphs entitled *Challenge-and-Response*
(where the ageless myth of an Encounter between two super-
human Beings is used as a main clue to the genesis of civilizations)
Toynbee[4] argues that the scandal of particularity is not really
avoided even by the astronomers in their account of the genesis
of our planetary system. He relies, of course, on the astronomy of
the time (1930), and too heavily, perhaps, on the brilliant pages
of Sir James Jeans, now somewhat outdated, apparently, by later
developments. Toynbee's main interest is in the theory that the
planets, including our earth, were thrown off from their parent
sun by the huge gravitational pull of a passing star as it 'wandered
blindly' through space some two thousand million years ago,
and that this was 'an event of almost unimaginable rarity'. His
somewhat unconvincing comment is that 'the rarity and the
momentousness of the event turn out to be almost as much of
the essence of the story as they are in the book of Genesis and in

---

[1] Cf. *The Philosophy of Symbolic Forms* by Ernst Cassirer (Yale, 1943), vol. I. Also his
Essay on Man (Yale, 1944), pp. 41f.: 'Instead of defining man as an *animal rationale* we
should define him as an *animal symbolicum*.'

[2] These now familiar terms 'nomothetic' and 'idiographic' are taken from Troeltsch
op. cit., and derive from Windelband's Rectorial Address at Strassburg in 1894. See also
Collingwood's survey of historiography from Herodotus to Croce in *The Idea of History*
(Oxford, 1956), pp. 14 – 204.

[3] From George Meredith's sonnet 'Lucifer in Starlight'.

[4] *A Study of History* (Oxford, 1934), I, 274 – 6.

he New Testament, where the encounters are between God and the Devil, and the consequences are the Fall and the Redemption of Man'. This is dubious because the particularity asserted in the scriptures is, as we have seen, strictly unique, whereas Sir James Jeans was arguing only for extreme rarity, and not for the possibility that life has appeared only on this planet (which is what Toynbee's suggestive parallel really requires). But whether or not this particularity is a legitimate inference from interstellar space, it seems to be the pattern of what has happened to the broad generalities of our terrestrial history. The generalities turn out to be progressively and selectively reduced. It is certain, wrote Professor C. C. J. Webb, 'that only one species of terrestrial life has attained to reason, only a small minority of that species to civilization, and only a minority of that minority to a civilization progressive and scientific'.[1]

It is the same pattern, though with a different use of materials, which appears in the biblical vision of world history as redemptive (*Heilsgeschichte*). The general truth that redemption will be universal, including the whole created order, is selectively represented and realized through a narrowing series of particularities – the whole Creation, Man, Israel, the faithful Remnant, the suffering Servant, Jesus the Christ – which thereafter becomes a widening series represented and realized by the Apostles, the Church, redeemed Humanity, redeemed Creation.[2]

In brief, particularity rather than generality is the prevailing structure of all our experience. It is certainly the structure of our religious experience. That God is omnipresent is a philosophical truth, the formal implicate of all ontological discourse. But it is not, as such, religious truth. That God is present in the sense that I am suddenly and overwhelmingly aware of his presence and know it to be inescapable – this alone has the dynamism of real experience. But, so far from being common and general it is rare and special; and I cannot know the times of its visitation.

[1] *J.T.S.* XLIV, 250, as quoted by C. H. Dodd, *The Bible Today* (Cambridge, 1943), p. 107.

[2] Cf. Oscar Cullmann, *Christ and Time* (S.C.M. 1951), pp. 115 – 17.

This doctrine of the omnipresence of God – as though by necessity of his being He must be bound to every time and to every place, like a natural force pervading space – is a frigid invention of metaphysical speculation, entirely without religious import. Scripture knows nothing of it. Scripture knows no 'Omnipresence', neither the expression nor the meaning it expresses; it knows only the God who is where he wills to be, and is not where he wills not to be, the 'deus mobilis', who is no mere universally extended being, but an august mystery, that comes and goes, approaches and withdraws, has its time and hour, and may be far or near in infinite degrees, 'closer than breathing' to us or miles remote from us. The hours of his 'visitation' and his 'return' are rare and solemn occasions, different essentially not only from the 'profane' life of every day, but also from the calm confiding mood of the believer, whose trust is to live ever before the face of God. They are the topmost summits in the life of the Spirit. They are not only rare occasions, they must needs be so for our sakes, for no creature can bear often or for long the full nearness of God's majesty in its beatitude and in its awefulness.[1]

The second answer which the Christian apologist would make here is that the inexplicable particularity of the revelatory fact is something *given*, and has to be accepted as such. And here we face the fact of Israel. We cannot pretend to explain why the fateful destiny of hearing the word of God should have been peculiar to this particular people; but it was. We have already noticed that the stumbling-block of particularity is inherent in all historical revelation. For history consists of interpreted events, and an event is particular in that it happens *here* and not there, *now* and not then; it happens to *this* person or group, not to that. Particularity being the inevitable characteristic of historical revelation, it is surely indisputable that the revelation of God in history did come to this one people Israel in a way that was peculiar, distinctive, momentous. Its destiny as God's 'chosen people' means that it was the sacramental nation; the bearer, in a uniquely effective sense, of a certain revelation. From no other source, save One, has the world received the living God as it has received him here. To ask 'why' is to ask the wrong question.

> Wisdom will repudiate thee if thou think to enquire
> *why* things are as they are, or whence they came; thy task
> is first to learn *what* is ....[2]

[1] Rudolf Otto, *The Idea of the Holy*; translated by J. W. Harvey (Oxford, 1926), who contributed Appendix VIII from which this quotation is taken.

[2] Robert Bridges, *The Testament of Beauty*.

Israel is God's 'what'. In Arthur Koestler's phrase she is humanity's 'exposed nerve'. This could be interpreted of her notorious sufferings through the centuries, as though they were the epitome and enduring monument of 'the giant agony of the world'. But Israel is humanity's exposed nerve in the deeper sense that here, more than anywhere else, Man's living awareness of the living God has declared and vindicated itself. For the very historical survival of the Jews as a people, in spite of unparalleled disasters, is a monument not to their faith in themselves but to their faith in God. 'They have stood beside the graves of all their oppressors in turn.' And this survival of a landless people, across long centuries, through knowledge of God, is the meaning of Disraeli's famous reply to Queen Victoria when she asked him what, in his opinion, is the real proof of the existence of God. 'Oh, the Jews, your Majesty.'

He was appealing to the objectivity of fact, the actuality inherent in 'doing the truth'. We may use a great journalist's dictum 'Comment is free; facts are sacred' to observe that here is a fact which is sacred in the most exact and literal sense. 'He hath not dealt so with any nation.'[1] His dealings here were nothing less than a gift of himself to humanity which Christendom will remember for ever as *praeparatio evangelica*.

The third answer which the Christian apologist would make here begins with a caveat; a warning lest the particularity of the biblical witness should be misinterpreted. To be the chosen people involved no mere favouritism; Israel was not 'teacher's pet', even though some Israelites cherished this illusion. In that passage already quoted from the prophet Amos the words 'you only have I known of all the families of the earth' are followed immediately by 'therefore I will punish you for your iniquities'. Election is not only to grace but to special responsibility. It is to the elect nation herself, therefore, that the prophetic word of penal judgment comes. To be humanity's exposed nerve, in the sense of being in covenant relationship with God, is to be exposed

[1] Ps. cxlvii. 20.

91

immediately and continuously to his Word, and to the momentous consequences of responding to it, or not responding.

The seer in the Apocalypse (v. 3 – 4) 'wept much because no man was able' to open the book and to loose the seals thereof; and his words recall the historic fact that no nation was able, not even Israel, consciously called though she was to stand in a specially vital relationship to God, and through the very particularity of that vocation to be the sacramental nation, symbolizing and mediating the final truth about God's judging and redeeming righteousness to all humanity.

It is easy to assume that the concept 'chosen people' was necessarily an expression of that national arrogance which is writ large in history; but Israel's prophets knew that this high vocation included the permanent threat of rejection and destruction. Indeed, it was more than a threat. It included the demand that Israel should accept destruction in order that God might do his strange work (Isa. xxviii. 21) through Israel (Isa. liii. 4 – 12), and so make actual his saving purpose for mankind.

As though in confirmation of this paradox the sublime climax of the religion of the Old Testament is the vision of the chosen people as God's suffering servant. It is very remarkable that the prophets could declare destruction to be Israel's fulfilment. They promised no happy ending to the story of the elect nation. Moreover, there is no happy ending, but a Cross, for the elect One, God's Messiah, whose perfect self-surrender and complete self-sacrifice are seen and declared by scripture to be the perfect, final revelation. The history of Israel at all its stages showed that the nation could not be the bearer of the revelation in this perfect, final, sense: this could happen only in a personal human life. It is the Christian claim that it did happen in the fulness of time, in a life which found its climax in the death of the Cross. It was this event which fulfilled the ancient expectations. This event is the centre of history: or, as Tillich has it, 'as its central event he creates the meaning of human history'.[1]

The Christian doctrine of the Incarnation concerns this event

---

[1] Op. cit. II, 96.

which happened. The doctrine is the attempted interpretation of the event. On the one hand it is an event with all the characteristics of a happening in time and space: it occurs once, ἅπαξ; it is unrepeatable; its form is special, individual and incomparable; it is the subject of historical report. On the other hand, history and faith alike testify that it is an event of universal significance, which may and must be interpreted in universal categories.

This vision of the universal through the offence of particularity brings us to the final point which the Christian apologist would make here: the climax and essence of his whole argument. The biblical witness to particularity is easily misunderstood and caricatured. What is its true intention and meaning?

A Master of Balliol once described the death of Socrates as having stopped the moral rot of Greece. It was doubtless a sound historical judgment. But why is it that the knowledge of this moving historical event will not arrest corruption now? Or, rather, what is it which isolates the Cross and makes it the solitary instance of time's irrelevance in the long history of martyrdom? Why does the dying of the Lord Jesus alone ignore the law of time's perspective, so that in the very particularity of this event there is a universal meaning?

We have described Israel as the 'sacramental' nation because this is the clue to human history used by the great prophets of the exile. Ezekiel, for example, knows that Jahweh is no tribal deity, but the true and only God whose writ runs everywhere: he is God of the whole earth. Yet Jahweh is also, and primarily, God of Israel; and though all the nations of the earth know him, they know him only as God of Israel.

But this has a very important meaning which is fully disclosed and articulated in the New Testament. It means that even though the revelation of God in history comes to one people only, the intention and meaning of such offensive particularity is that through this people it shall extend to all mankind. This very particularity is the sacrament of universality. It is one of the characteristic paradoxes of scripture that universality is the implicit logic of its strange particularity; 'God so loved the world' is the outcome, in fact as well as in theory, of what begins as 'You only have I known of all the families of the earth'.

The Bible is primarily concerned with the eternal God's dynamic disclosure of himself through certain events of time: it is a history book rather than a treatise on moral philosophy. It takes historic time seriously and tells a story. But this book is bound, as it were, within transcendental covers: it has a prologue and an epilogue which look beyond history, and are therefore presented in mythical form. Creation, Fall and Flood at the 'beginning', like Doomsday at the 'end', are the supra-historical framework within which the historical revelation (with all its baffling particularity) has to be understood.

I take what follows from Professor Dodd's illuminating pages in *The Bible Today*[1] where the great pre-historic and post-historic myths are shown to illustrate the recurrent, biblical theme of Judgment-and-Renewal.[2]

God's judgment comes upon man in disaster, but leads to a new creation, as in Genesis ix. 9 – 10. As Adam is all mankind, so is Noah; the story stands as a witness that God's covenant (though historically it was made with Israel) is applicable to the whole human race. The principles of divine action revealed in the history of a particular people are thus applied to *mankind*, at *all* times and in *all* places. These 'pre-historic' stories have the effect of universalizing the meaning of the story of the people of God. All mankind is comprehended in the fall of Adam, in the covenant with Noah, and in the Last Judgment.

Thus the supra-historical, mythical framework in which the historical revelation is set universalizes the meaning of the revelation given to particular people at particular times. I quote Professor Dodd's conclusion verbatim:

The Word which was spoken through the prophets of Israel and made flesh in Palestine in the first century, is the same Word by which man and his world were created, which is also the Agent of final judgement upon the quick and the dead, and the Mediator of eternal life to all men. It follows that whatever

[1] *The Bible To-day* (Cambridge, 1943), pp. 71, 107, 114 f., 118 f.
[2] See p. 10 above.

is said in Scripture about God's relations with men is not to be understood in any restrictive or exclusive sense. If the Bible records that God entered into covenant with Israel, or with the Church, by which he promised them certain blessings and laid upon them certain obligations, that is solid matter of fact, verifiable and datable in history. But it does not carry the inference that the rest of mankind is outside God's covenant, incapable of receiving his blessing, and under no obligation to him. On the contrary, we can be sure that God speaks to all men everywhere in judgement and mercy just because he did, verifiably, so speak to his 'chosen people' in history.[1]

God's revelation, then, is for all mankind. And this is why the Church is catholic; that is, universal. Ideally, it is the whole human race as redeemed through Christ; it is redeemed humanity *in nucleo*. The unity of all mankind in Christ is what the Church, the new Israel, means; indeed the Church is meaningless unless, in the end, it is universal. And so we come to the Church as the redeemed Society, which is the theme of the following chapter.

APPENDIX

In this chapter the problem raised by the particularist emphasis of scripture has been discussed mainly within the context of man's earth-bound history. We have hardly touched on the cosmic aspect of the problem, the relation of Christ to the universe, which is the concern of the later epistles of St Paul, the epistle to the Hebrews and the Fourth Gospel. The problem, in this aspect, became specially acute when the geocentric cosmology had to be abandoned in the seventeenth century as erroneous: the earth could no longer be conceived of as the centre of the universe. As 'one of a myriad myriad floating specks of dust', was it chosen by God for 'the scene of the unique divine event'?[2] What of the other specks?

Here, where all thought is speculative, we may refer to what has been written respectively by the most distinguished living exponent of philosophical theology, and by a distinguished poet.

(i) Tillich's answer[3] leaves the universe

---

[1] *Op. cit.* p. 119.

[2] Toynbee, *A Study of History*, I, 275.

[3] *Systematic Theology*, II, 96.

open for possible divine manifestations in other areas or periods of being. Such possibilities cannot be denied. But they cannot be proved or disproved. Incarnation is unique for the special group in which it happens, but it is not unique in the sense that other singular incarnations for other unique worlds are excluded. Man cannot claim that the infinite has entered the finite to overcome its existential estrangement in mankind alone. Man cannot claim to occupy the only possible place for Incarnation . . . .

Perhaps one can go a step further. The interdependence of everything with everything else in the totality of being includes a participation of nature in history and demands a participation of the universe in salvation. Therefore, if there are non-human 'worlds' in which existential estrangement is not only real – as it is in the whole universe – but in which there is also a type of awareness of this estrangement, such worlds cannot be without the operation of saving power within them . . . . The manifestation of saving power in one place implies that saving power is operating in all places. The expectation of the Messiah as the bearer of the New Being presupposes that 'God loves the universe', even though in the appearance of the Christ he actualizes this love for historical man alone.

(ii) Here is Alice Meynell's answer:

> With this ambiguous earth
> His dealings have been told us. These abide:
> The signal to a maid, the human birth,
> The lesson, and the young Man crucified.

> But not a star of all
> The innumerable host of stars has heard
> How He administered this terrestrial ball.
> Our race have kept their Lord's entrusted Word.

> Of His earth-visiting feet
> None knows the secret, cherished, perilous,
> The terrible, shamefast, frightened, whispered, sweet,
> Heart-shattering secret of His way with us.

> No planet knows that this
> Our wayside planet, carrying land and wave,
> Love and life multiplied, and pain and bliss,
> Bears, as chief treasure, one forsaken grave.

> Nor, in our little day,
> May His devices with the heavens be guessed,
> His pilgrimage to thread the Milky Way,
> Or His bestowals there be manifest.

But in the eternities
Doubtless we shall compare together, hear
A million alien Gospels, in what guise
He trod the Pleiades, the Lyre, the Bear.

O be prepared, my soul!
To read the inconceivable, to scan
The million forms of God those stars unroll
When, in our turn, we show to them a Man.[1]

[1] 'Christ in the Universe', from *The Poems of Alice Meynell* (Burns Oates, 1924),p . 92.

CHAPTER VI

THE REDEEMED SOCIETY

He habitually wrote not 'I' but 'we', and his 'we' was no crowd or sect, but humankind. That humble inheritance included none of the splendours of recorded civilization, but it did include Adam's dignity, his fall, his exile and his hope of salvation. As a poet he felt himself to be the heir of the unrecorded memories of many lives, human and pre-human. His themes were archetypal; ... present history he also experienced as his own. The sufferings of the modern world moved him deeply; for the doctrinaire communist worker on some collective farm in Czechoslovakia was still Adam, obscured in a cloud of dust.[1]

In these words, taken from her appreciation of Edwin Muir a few days after his death early in 1959, Kathleen Raine says three things about poetry in our time which are also distinctive of modern theology. The true Christian understanding of man is corporate rather than individualist in its emphasis. Further, its presupposition is the corporate life of all humanity: if the Church is not universal in the sense that it is redeemed humanity *in nucleo* it is ultimately meaningless. Further, though the Church is an objective order of life given in history, it transcends history; its thought and language are archetypal; the deeps of its supernatural life may be sounded only in symbol and sacrament; baptism and eucharist are sacraments of redemption by which the redeemed sons of Adam recapitulate the conflict and victory of the Second Adam.

In thinking about man in society we are obviously concerned with the supreme issue of our age. That it is the ultimate issue for modern man is already a commonplace. We belong to an epoch of history in which something unprecedented and unique is happening. It has never happened on our planet before. The whole living generation of mankind is being knit together by modern technical science into a single world society. A world in

[1] *The Listener* (B.B.C., London), 15 January 1959.

98

which microphone and television camera can link anyone anywhere with anyone else anywhere else is not only a small world; it is already one world. This is the new fact confronting man; and he cannot help speculating, grimly, about the character and pattern of the coming one-world society. What will life in it be for his children?

A more relevant question, perhaps, is Plato's: 'What kind of citizens do we want our children to be?' It was part of Plato's genius that he asked the questions that matter; and this is the one which now matters supremely. What *kind* of world community? We may recall the story of the Greek soldier who was taken prisoner and questioned by his captors. 'Of what πόλις (city) are you?', they asked. And he, with courageous prescience, replied, 'I am κοσμοπολίτης (a citizen of the world)'. It was a fine but pathetic attempt to achieve an ideal which is now thrust upon us as a fact. What will this fact mean for our grandchildren in 2000 A.D.?

It would be a lazy simplification to suggest that it will mean a choice between two polar opposites: a totalitarian ant-heap on the one hand and individualistic anarchy on the other. But we may begin, as they do in the artillery, by 'bracketing' in this way, since man's thought about the possible patterns of social relationship is logically bounded by these two extreme positions. The relation of the individual to society is the enduring political problem, of course; it is a very old problem and it refuses facile solutions; yet most solutions tend to group themselves as one or other of two alternative types which we may label for convenience the individualist and the collectivist. Individualism means the self-affirmation of the individual as such without too much regard for his relation to the world around. Collectivism means the affirmation of the self only as part of a larger whole, and without too much regard for the self's inherent individuality. These are abstractions, admittedly, from the variety and complexity of concrete situations in real life; they are useful nevertheless. As necessary prolegomena to the Christian understanding of society as redeemed, we have to look at them here.

I

Individualism asserts that human personality is inherently 'self-centred'. This is not, as yet, an adverse value-judgment but a statement of fact. A human person is a self, and that self is unique, incomparable, separate, self-determining and free: it is something unrepeatable and irreplaceable: even though it can be destroyed by violence, its ultimate inviolability cannot be. The self *as self* is basic fact, lying below all moral evaluations of what it does with its selfhood. Though centred in itself in the psychological sense it is not necessarily, and not yet, 'self-centred' in the moral sense. This has to be emphasized at the outset if only because it has to be virtually contradicted in the sequel. As Tillich insists, 'separation is not estrangement, self-centredness is not selfishness, self-determination is not sinfulness. . . . It is time to end the bad theological usage of jumping with moral indignation on every word in which the syllable 'self' appears. Even moral indignation would not exist without a centred self and ontological self-affirmation.'[1]

But if the self is a fact, 'selves' are a fact – an innumerable plurality of different centres of finite consciousness co-existing in this universe which God has made. Each self is a universe reflecting the whole universe 'in a peculiar mode' (Leibniz), and existing alongside innumerable similar selves, no one of them setting boundaries to the potential infinitude of another, and each one of them having its own individual relation to God. It was in order to conceive and state this mystery philosophically that Leibniz invoked the principle of 'pre-established harmony'; and this was the accepted philosophical justification of individualism and liberalism in the eighteenth and nineteenth centuries.

To Immanuel Kant, another of the founding fathers of our modern liberalism, a man's freedom means sovereignty over himself: it is the right to obey a self-imposed imperative of duty. And because a man's freedom is exercised not in a vacuum but in society, Kant added that this right to be a person necessarily

[1] *The Courage to Be* (Nisbet, 1955), p. 82.

involves treating other people as persons: that is, not as mere means to the ends of others, but as ends in themselves. The very claim to the rights of personality is *eo ipso* the duty to recognize them in others. It is what 'pre-established harmony' makes possible and means.

In theory and ideally the freedom of each individual person as something sacred and inviolable *can* work out harmoniously in society: more than an abstract possibility, it has been and still is the driving force in all that is best in Western democracy. But an ideal can be exploited and corrupted in this fallen world order; and the best, when corrupted, becomes the worst. The Kantian doctrine of freedom worked out in fact, and on the broad field of modern civilized life, not as harmony but as *laissez-faire* and the notorious economics of capitalist industrialism, with the result that the individual selfhood of industrial man, so far from being free and self-determining, was manipulated and used as a mere object in a world of objects. In the coalmines and factories of nineteenth-century Britain men, women and children were not treated as ends in themselves but as means to the mercenary ends of the *entrepreneur*. The slum dwellings of the midlands and the north are still a dreary monument to freedom as interpreted by the Manchester school of Cobden and Bright. For multitudes, a divinely pre-established harmony turned out to be 'every man for himself, and the devil take the hindmost'.

It is not surprising, therefore, that the victims of the Industrial Revolution, particularly the proletarian masses of Western Europe in the nineteenth century, repudiated individualism and the 'bourgeois ideology' of pre-established harmony which was its theoretical justification. The derogatory Marxist use of the term 'ideology' is modern, but ideology as an attempt to preserve existing evils by a doctrine of divine providence which justifies them is very old; it is writ large in history. On the threshold of our modern period it was illustrated cynically by Voltaire who stopped an atheistic conversation at his dinner-table until the butler should have left the room, and then explained that he had done so out of concern for his silver. In England the reactionary era which followed the French Revolution saw the *élite* affecting more patience with forms of religion they no longer believed in because those forms had desirable social effects; desirable, that is, for themselves. The Duke of Wellington went to church, as he put it, 'to set a good example to the common people'. Had it been his only reason it would have been a bad reason: a religious establishment which serves the interests of a privileged minority is the opium of the masses, as many besides Marx and Engels have noticed. 'Aristocracies', wrote a Camden professor of ancient history at Oxford, 'spring from economic distinctions and fortify themselves by an appeal to religion.'[1]

With the triumphant rise of the middle classes to power throughout the nineteenth century the days of aristocratic privilege were numbered; but the communists of 1848 saw the same abuse in the new bourgeois ideology of 'the sacred freedom of the individual'. Marx could hardly have asked for a more damningly naïve interpretation of it than that provided by Höffding's philosophy of religion when the liberal era was reaching its climax in the early twentieth century. Höffding defined religion as 'the conservation of socially recognized values', without staying to consider, apparently, whose social recognition is to bestow this *cachet* of value. For there are, in fact, different values at different times and for different classes of society: they are in some sense relative to the differing social and economic circumstances of those who embody them – as Doolittle reminds us in Shaw's *Pygmalion*: 'middle class morality claims its victim.' John Oman's shrewd comment on Höffding is that true and living religion is concerned with *judging* the values which *ought* to be conserved.[2]

This critical comment takes us a step further. For abuse does not invalidate use: it calls for judgment and change; a right use of a valid principle rather than its outright rejection. And in spite of distortions and corruptions of the ideal of pre-established harmony, Western man still refuses to belittle the fact of personal individuality which gave rise to the ideal. After all, his indivi-

[1] I owe the substance and wording of parts of this paragraph to a source which I am unable to trace.
[2] *The Natural and the Supernatural* (Cambridge, 1931), p. 306. My italics.

dualism is not a thing of yesterday: it emerged notably at the Renaissance as a protest against collectivism, both that of the ancient world and its feudal counterpart in the world of the middle ages. But it has rarely if ever left itself without witness, and this for two reasons: the great collectivist stabilities of history are always being undermined by the two ineluctable facts that make man Man.

The first is a physical fact. Man's physical body is not only the locus (in some sense) but also the expression and safeguard of his individuality.[1] The dictator can standardize life and even thought from cradle to grave within his slave-state, until the slaves become mere tiddly-winks for political opportunism to play with; he can wash their brains, poison their minds and mesmerize them into mass action 'as one man'. Yet just there the totalitarian techniques of his brave new world reach their limit, since he cannot fuse those who act *as* one man *into* one man: he cannot merge them into a single obedient robot. Such fusion is beyond the reach of the most absolute power. Persons, however much standardized as 'things', have still to be born separately and to die separately. The 'memory' of birth and the expectation of death give to every human being an indefeasible separateness: man's physical structure involves an individuality which is inalienable.

The second is a moral fact. Man's moral structure expresses and safeguards his individuality. The sense of guilt is the great guardian of personal identity. It is the *shameful* me (Luther's *ich schadhaft*) which will never allow me to doubt or escape my separate, continuous, responsible, personal being. The most rigidly cohesive social structures known to history disintegrate at last under the disturbing pressures of inalienable personal responsibility and personal guilt. Ancient Israel provides a pertinent example here. The thought of the ancient Hebrews was strongly collectivist. The dominant and enduring reality was Israel, rather than this or that individual Israelite. All issues were communal, including moral issues. Group suffered for individual misdeeds and individual for group misdeeds. The successive generations

[1] See p. 155 below.

had one and the same organic unity. As the proverb put it: It is the children's teeth that are set on edge when the fathers have eaten sour grapes. Yet there comes a moment when the prophet Ezekiel in his eighteenth chapter attacks this in the name of the isolated, responsible, guilty individual. 'What mean ye that ye use this proverb concerning Israel, saying, The fathers have eaten sour grapes and the children's teeth are set on edge? As I live saith the Lord God, ye shall not have occasion any more to use this proverb in Israel. Behold . . . the soul that sinneth, *it* shall die. . . . The son shall not bear the iniquity of the father . . . the righteousness of the righteous shall be upon *him*, and the wickedness of the wicked shall be upon *him*.'[1]

To these two facts a third must be added as soon as we look more particularly at Christendom and its history. A high estimate of the individual person is implicit in the gospel, and has always been explicit in its proclamation. 'Are not two sparrows sold for a farthing'; that is, so cheap that you cannot buy them separately? But the Father knows and values each individually: he does not see them even in pairs; not one falls to the ground without him.[2] Or those ninety and nine sheep – does he not leave them, and go out after the one?[3]

> And none of the ransomed ever knew
>> How deep were the waters crossed;
> Nor how dark was the night that the Lord passed through,
>> Till he found the sheep that was lost.

'Sheep, so much alike that you and I make no difference between the singular and the plural; but to the Good Shepherd there are no "sheep"; there is only this sheep and that.'[4]

This is not the only witness which the Christian religion makes here: it has a further, complementary witness to which we now have to turn. But the fact which remains, and which there is no gainsaying, is that the Christian religion is incompatible with any form of totalitarian thought or practice which would absorb the

[1] Ezek. xviii. 2 – 4, 20. My italics.
[2] Mat. x. 29.
[3] Mat. xviii. 11 – 13.
[4] R. A. Knox, *Sermons* (privately printed), p. 77

person into the mass as though he were a mere instance of a class. In a true and necessary sense its witness is individualist.

II

There has long been an emphasis complementary to all this if not actually opposed to it: the collective emphasis. Here the accent is not so much on the individual as on the group in its organic unity. Plato's *Republic* idealized the regimented society, and Aristotle's *Politics* distilled from the rich diversity of Greek history the uniform testimony that man is a 'political animal'.[1] From that classical testimony right down to Hegel's virtual apotheosis of the state and the actual apotheosis assumed by the police-states of our own time, voices repudiating mere individualism as atomistic, anarchic and, in fact, unreal, have never been wanting. They have disallowed the concept of the isolated individual. Their emphasis has been on the inescapable unity, the organic togetherness, of truly human life. Even in our Western world, so long dominated by the individualism of the Renaissance, this philosophy of the corporate in its various forms has been gaining momentum for over a century. It was reaffirmed in England by Burke and Coleridge. It is a 'solidary' or 'societary' rather than an atomistic conception of man, for it asserts that personality is mutual in its very being. For all its sovereign individuality, a self comes to be only in a community of selves.[2] We may illustrate this from the three related fields of economics, philosophy and psychology.

First, economics. In the second book of the *Republic* Plato argued for the state as a natural necessity against the Sophists who asserted its artificiality. For them it was no part of the natural order (φύσις) but an arbitrary convention (νόμος), whereas for Plato the state is part of the given order of things because a man is never self-dependent. To be a man at all he needs community. As an 'economic' being the individual depends on the services of other individuals; their lives could not be truly human without a state to live in.

[1] *Politics* I, i.
[2] I have discussed this in *The Protestant Tradition* (Cambridge, 1955), pp. 218 – 19.

Second, philosophy. Here Kant elaborated an important parallel argument, starting from reason as man's distinctive endowment. It is a peculiarity of reason that it cannot be fully developed within the lifetime of the single individual. Because he is rational, and has the faculty of profiting by the experience of others, the full development of his powers requires an historical process. Collingwood discusses what he describes as 'Kant's remarkable feat of showing why there should be such a thing as history' and adds:

No one can invent the whole of mathematics out of his own head. . . . If what you want is food, the fact that another cow has eaten a certain blade of grass only prevents you from eating that blade; but if what you want is knowledge, the fact that Pythagoras has discovered the theorem about the square on the hypotenuse gives that piece of knowledge to you more easily than you could have got it for yourself. Consequently the purpose of nature for the development of man's reason is a purpose that can be fully realized only in the history of the human race and not in an individual life. . . . (Plato shows that) as an economic being man must have a state to live in; similarly Kant shows that, as a rational being, he must have an historical process to live in.[1]

Third, psychology. Here we may begin with the apostle, who knew that we are members one of another (Eph. iv. 25). This is more than ancient Stoic formula or modern socialist nostrum; it is the structural pattern of all personal life. As Socrates urged against Glaucon, an individual self, considered in isolation from its environment, is an abstraction, not a really existing thing; and modern psychology has elaborated this, teaching us how complex personality is. It is not the endowment which the individual possesses from the start, such as red hair, or an aptitude for mathematics. It is something which grows out of his relationships with others. It comes only in the communion of personal encounter. In Martin Buber's famous sentence, 'I find my being in you (or 'I become myself up against you'); all real life is meeting.'[2] To those who are in love this needs no demonstration. The lover finds his true being only in the beloved; each knows the other as *animae dimidium meae* (one-half of my very life).[3] When one

---

[1] *The Idea of History* (Oxford, 1956), p. 98.
[2] *Ich werde am Du: alles wirkliche Leben ist Begegnung.*
[3] Horace, *Odes* I, iii, 8. See St Augustine's use of this in *Confessions* IV, vi.

refers to the other as 'my better half' it is love's tribute to this mystery of individuality through togetherness.

We live as 'economic' and rational beings, then, only in society and in the historic continuity of its life. Only in society, indeed, do we become persons at all. The self comes to be only in a community of selves. Tom, Dick and Harry are names standing for separate and sovereign individualities, admittedly: yet Tom is Tom only as he presupposes the others and meets them in the triangular tension of mutual co-operation and resistance. Man's seeming separateness is half an illusion, therefore, since it is as much a product of community as an ingredient of community.

Further, it is a continuous product. Not only do we *become* persons in community; it is only in continuous encounter with others that we *remain* persons in the genuine and full sense. This is one reason why prolonged solitary confinement is so terrible a punishment. It threatens its victim with mental derangement, the break-up of the normally unified self. It is a form of death; or, rather, a prolonged dying to which actual death is preferable (hence the French *s'ensevelir dans la solitude*). This, too, is the reason why the solitary hermit in his cell is no healthy or true expression of the genius of Christianity. The Christian doctrine of the Church witnesses to the fact that faith is life, indefeasibly corporate and social.

It seems, then, that the familiar antithesis between individualism and collectivism is facile and misleading. It presents the relation between the self and its world as a clear-cut distinction, a contrast between 'inside' and 'outside'. This contrast may describe the individuality of a pebble separated from the neighbouring cliff; but the world of mind differs from the world of nature, and metaphors of 'sundering' and 'separation' express a half-truth at best. For the self is a self only because it has a world to which it belongs and from which it is separated at the same time. Individuality has participation as its correlative. Tillich's definition of participation[1] is 'being a part of something from which

---

[1] *The Courage to Be*, p. 83.

one is, at the same time, separated'. It is Plato's μέθεξις, the partici-pation by earthly objects in the heavenly Ideas which are eternally distinct therefrom; the *relation* of the individual to the universal.

In the world of religion this universal is always realized through the community of the group. Primitive man opposes to the fact of death his confidence in the solidarity, the unbroken and in-destructible unity of life. The social relations of human beings extend far beyond the furthest possible range of their personal relations, and this is strikingly evident in primitive societies. Just as in any society at almost any moment the majority of its mem-bers are already dead, so in a primitive tribe the 'Ancestors' com-prise many more generations than the recent one with which some of its present members have overlapped. And it is through his conscious social nexus with the Ancestors that the sacred sanctions of tribal customs are vitally conserved for primitive man. Indeed, his totems express and convey his kinship and com-munity with *all* living beings.[1]

In religion at a higher level revelation is originally given and received in and through the struggles and self-surrender of a personal life. But, again, no individual is deemed to receive such a revelation for himself alone; he receives it within and for his group and, by implication, for all groups; for all mankind.

The classic illustration here is the vocation of the prophets of Israel. The prophet mediates the revelation to the group which 'belongs' to him as he belongs to it. Further, Israel's prophet *par excellence*, the long-expected Messiah, is never conceived of simply as an isolated individual but as a messianic community which appears with him and which he in some sense embodies. The messianic concept is always 'Messiah plus Community' in vital unity. He is inseparably related to an imperishable community which transcends temporal limitation, the tense distinction of past, present and future becoming virtually irrelevant.[2] Thus his function as redeemer is not so much to save individuals, and not

[1] Ernst Cassirer, *An Essay on Man* (Doubleday, New York, 1953), pp. 114 f., where he also quotes Robertson Smith's *The Religion of the Semites* (Edinburgh, 1889), pp. 53 ff. and 334 ff.

[2] See p. 145 below.

at all to withdraw them singly out of historical existence into an eternal order (as in Platonism): his function is to transform historical existence itself by being the instrument and embodiment of a 'new creation', the kingdom of God.

Thus, our Christian knowledge of God has been made possible, and is only possible now, through and in the Community which has had a continuous existence from the beginning 'in Christ' ('before Abraham was I am'): it is the imperishable community of the Body of Christ. The New Testament describes it as the fellowship of the Holy Spirit. To be a Christian is to be one of Christ's people, the people of God, the old Israel made new in and through the Cross and Resurrection of God's Son, and destined to reach its full and perfect stature only when all humanity – past, present and future – is redeemed.

The standardized evangelism of the past hundred years – familiar to the English-speaking world through the successive campaigns of Talmadge, Moody, Booth, Torrey, Graham and others – has preached Christ too exclusively in terms of the isolated individual and his personal destiny, as though the gospel were primarily a private matter concerning himself alone. This aspect of the gospel is not untrue, as a work of genius, *The Pilgrim's Progress*, suffices to remind us: no one can take my place in the secret place; I cannot reach the celestial city by proxy. But this is a precious aspect of the gospel rather than the 'full gospel' which it is often alleged to be. Indeed, it can be a new form of egoism which would make Christ himself the ally of the individual's inveterate self-centredness; so that what purports to be properly inward and spiritual is, in fact, dangerously private and self-regarding. The new salvation can be the old sin writ large, and a pertinent commentary on the most frequently attested of Christ's sayings in the gospels, 'he that saveth his life shall lose it'.

The fact is, as the old and serious man said to John Wesley, that 'the scriptures know nothing of solitary religion'. The thought of the New Testament about our redemption is truly personal in that it is corporate and communal rather than individual and private. It is expressed in the great imagery of Body and members, Vine and branches, the fellowship of the Spirit, the one Loaf, the communion of the Body of Christ. In short, its concern is with the common life of the Lord's Body, symbolized and conveyed in the Christian Sacraments, announced and made actual in Christian ethics. 'Christians should be the last people found clinging to the wrecks of an atomistic individualism which has no foundation in the Bible.'[1]

Authentic Christian life, so far from being atomistic in structure or action, has the unity of the organism. For just as my sin involves and expresses a triple estrangement, (i) from God, (ii) from and within myself as made in his image, and (iii) from my neighbour: so my redemption involves and expresses a triple reconciliation, (i) with God, (ii) within my proud, self-loving, self-worshipping soul, 'curved inwards upon itself', and (iii) with my neighbour whom I have been exploiting as an object rather than meeting as a person. And this God-given reconciliation with my neighbours – my fellow sinners whose rebellions and exploitings match mine, and whose lives interlock with mine to form a vast network of evil – this is the constitutive fact of the new life in Christ. His work of reconciliation re-establishes not only our filial relation to God but, at the same time, our fraternal relation to one another. One of the earliest names for the Church was the Brotherhood (ἡ ἀδελφότης).

III

The New Testament document which gathers all this up and states it, not as theological doctrine or ethical ideal but as something which authenticated itself in historic fact and went on to change the course of world history, is the book of The Acts of the Apostles.

In the preface to his commentary on this book Calvin has a short way with the pseudepigraphical literature of the early Church, apocryphal Acts and the like, 'stinking trifles that cause the wicked to laugh at them and the godly to loathe them'.

[1] J. A. T. Robinson, *The Body* (S.C.M. 1953), p. 9.

To-day we look more charitably and seriously at these 'novels with a religious purpose', as Canon Streeter called them, and realize that even beneath the story of Thecla or the *Clementine Recognitions* there may be some historical basis.

But Calvin was fundamentally right when he turned from such a mingle-mangle (*farrago*) to this memoir (*monumentum*) by St Luke, 'wherein is depicted in most lively fashion the beginning and also the increasing of the Church of Christ', and beside which 'the feigned disputation of Peter with Simon Magus is a filthy toy'.

He was right, because Acts is both memoir and monument. In form as well as in substance it is unique. We have nothing like it again for two hundred and fifty years. Without Acts (even though it leaves us with unsolved and perhaps insoluble problems) the classic beginnings of Christianity would be a door locked and the key lost, and only the keyhole to peep at.

A valid description of this precious document would be the story of original Christianity in action: and yet its author would have summarized it differently. To him it was the story of the new action of God in human history. As we have already noticed,[1] this his second treatise is dominated by the fact of the Spirit. The Church, the new community of the Spirit, is the authentication of the new era of the Messiah, the new creation. That which was spoken of by the prophets has come to pass, and *now is*. What was it? The answer is given in that *locus classicus*, the story of Pentecost.

When the day of Pentecost had come they were all together in one place. And suddenly a sound came from heaven like the rush of a mighty wind, and it filled all the house where they were sitting. And there appeared to them tongues as of fire, distributed and resting on each one of them. And they were all filled with the Holy Spirit and began to speak in other tongues as the Spirit gave them utterance ... (Acts ii. 1 – 4, R.S.V.).

What does this mean? Plainly this sound like wind would provide no statistics for the meteorological office: nor could these tongues of fire have been photographed by the cameras of modern pressmen. St Luke's primary purpose here is interpretation rather than description. He wishes to make clear that neither the

[1] See p. 15 above.

confusion of tongues at Babel, nor the giving of the sacred Law itself on Sinai, were as historically momentous as this baptism of the Church by wind and fire at Pentecost. He is depicting the lordship of the risen Redeemer in the Church of his Body; the redeemed community of the Holy Spirit. It is his meditative historical sense which makes the author of Acts aware that this community of the Spirit is what being 'in Christ' means. Here is the distinctive character, the essential and enduring operation, of Christian life and experience. Here is the new life in its indubitable reality; as much an objective fact in the world of the spirit as is a prairie fire or a hurricane in the world of nature. It is given to wayfaring men and received by them. It comes upon them from outside themselves, invading, controlling and transforming their common life.

Treating him as a photographer rather than as an artist, as a chronicler rather than as an historian, St Luke's critics have often pointed to details in his classic picture of the birthday of the Church which are out of focus. Speaking with tongues, for example. They observe that the contemporary witness of St Paul is more trustworthy and more convincing. His letters show that 'tongues' could not have meant a dozen foreign languages, severally heard and understood by members of a cosmopolitan crowd (*vv*. 5 – 13), who proceeded at once to make a detailed list of them with the sober precision of a passport office. Speaking with tongues (*glossolalia*), they rightly observe, is a phenomenon not uncommon in the history of religion: as the accompaniment of a mood of intense spiritual exaltation it happened within living memory during the Welsh revival. When it happened at the first Christian Pentecost in Jerusalem it sounded to cynical bystanders like inarticulate babbling, and they said as much. 'These men have been drinking.' But St Paul, who himself claims to have received this psychic gift on rare occasions, knew it to be a form of religious ecstasy which communicated its meaning to others similarly gifted, across the usual barriers of foreign race and speech. Indeed, he was somewhat afraid of it as something extravagant and dangerous. He tells the Corinthians that to have this gift – even to be possessed and caught up into the third heaven by it – is ultimately irrelevant to the Christian man's main concern. He deprecates paying undue attention to it. What matters, he says, is its meaning and outcome for daily living. The sound, the flame, the ecstasy of poetic speech, are less important than the integrity and dependability of the Christian life which they dramatically illustrate: those fruits of the Spirit which are love, joy, peace, righteousness, long-suffering, self-control. If any man be in Christ he is a new man, in that sense: he is a new creation. Old desires have passed away. Their energy has taken a new direction. Individual life has found a new centre of gravity, and so found itself, in a transformed social life. And what he says about 'tongues', therefore, would seem to apply to the sound like a hurricane and the lambent fire.

Such criticism is doubtless sound and necessary. By bringing facts to a proper focus it dismisses fables to their proper obscurity. But history is always more than bare fact. It is interpreted fact, the vertebral structure of event clothed with the living flesh of meaning. And if symbolic myth or legend be indispensable to that meaning, it is as much 'historical' as is the evidence of cameras and tape-recorders.[1] St Luke's conscious artistry, in terms of ancient legends about Babel and Sinai, is historical interpretation more relevant than the evidence of mocking eye-witnesses whose only clue to 'joy in the Holy Spirit' is 'drinking before breakfast' (*vv*. 13 and 15).

How, then, does the author of Acts understand and interpret Pentecost? The answer is mainly twofold.

First, Pentecost is Babel in reverse, so to speak. This is a motif which we meet in the evangelist's earlier volume; his Gospel opens with it. There the good news of man's redemption is announced from heaven itself by the angels of God who say 'Fear not. Behold I bring you good tidings of great joy which shall be unto all people. ... Glory to God in the highest.' But this 'Fear not ... glory be to God on high' recalls and answers the precisely opposite theme in the ancient legend of Babel; namely, man's

---

[1] See pp. 32 and 38 above.

anxious fear and the idolatrous self-assertion which goes with it.

> Now the whole earth had one language and few words.... Then they said, 'Come, let us build ourselves a city, and a tower with its top in the heavens, and let us make a name for ourselves, lest we be scattered abroad upon the face of the whole earth'. And the Lord came down to see the city and the tower, which the sons of men had built. And the Lord said, 'Behold, they are one people, and they have all one language; and this is only the beginning of what they will do; and nothing that they propose to do will now be impossible for them. Come, let us go down, and there confuse their language, that they may not understand one another's speech'. So the Lord scattered them abroad from there over the face of all the earth, and they left off building the city. Therefore its name was called Babel (Gen. xi. 1, 4 – 9, R.S.V.).

The meaning and universal relevance of this is that when men's hearts are failing them for fear of that which may be coming upon the earth, they build their towers of Babel and cry, as Swinburne did, 'Glory to man in the highest, for man is the master of things'. It is a self-sufficiency which betrays a deep-seated anxiety.[1] The *hubris* which will know no security for man save in his own technological achievements (bigger and better bombs) occurs in a world situation of deepening moral perversity which gives it the lie.

But for St Luke it is Gospel, Good News, that the misdirection of all human life, of which Babel is the symbol, is met by the redeeming activity of God, of which Pentecost is the symbol. The estranging confusion of tongues is done away by the miracle of reconciliation and unity in the community of the Spirit, the One Body of the risen Christ.

Rabbinic tradition had declared that in the beginning men had one speech, intelligible to all, the effective symbol of their divinely intended unity. This primitive language was confounded by the sin of pride at Babel; the divisions and barriers of history are the result. But there would come at last in the fulness of time God's reversal of man's tragic predicament; an end of his suicidal disunity; the breaking-down of the barriers which have destroyed human community in every generation. 'Ye shall become one people of the Lord and one tongue; and there shall no longer be

---

[1] Cf. *The Protestant Tradition*, pp. 33 – 6.

the spirit of deceit, and of Beliar' (*Testament of the Twelve Patri-archs*).

Speaking with tongues, therefore, which every man in that cosmopolitan crowd might understand and share was nothing less than the fulfilment of this age-long hope. It was the long-expected divine gift of the Spirit, breaking down barriers and ending man's immemorial alienation from his fellows. This, says St Luke, is the meaning of the birthday of the Church and of its world-wide mission, in time and beyond time. The Church of God is destined to include all humanity. Its meaning lies in its ultimate universality.

In the second place, St Luke knew that this miracle of speaking and hearing inevitably recalled the parallel divine activity on Mount Sinai, centuries before. The reference was inescapable. Pentecost was a harvest festival celebrated once a year, but to every true son of Israel it was much more. It was the anniversary day of thanksgiving not only for the covenanted bounty of God in the harvest field, but also for the gift of his sacred Law on Sinai, itself the meaning and covenant expression of a righteousness which redeems.

According to tradition the feast of Pentecost was the day on which the Law had been announced at Sinai by the divine voice from heaven. Indeed, the Jews gathered in Jerusalem on the first Whit Sunday were there primarily for this sacrifice of praise and thanksgiving. Along with the great commemorative feast of the Passover this, too, was Israel's way of recalling and celebrating the most wonderful of her days of old: her greatest historic moment, her sublimest covenant experience: namely, her exodus from the house of bondage in Egypt, and the effective sign and seal of this deliverance, God's announcement of the covenant Law to his awestruck people at the holy mountain.

Further, the giving of this sacred Torah of judgment and redemption on Sinai was marked by wonders similar to those described here by St Luke: an intelligible divine Voice, and fire. The scriptures of the old covenant constantly recall this mighty act of God.

For the Lord thy God is a merciful God. He will not forsake thee, neither destroy thee, nor forget the covenant of thy fathers which he sware unto them. . . . Did ever people hear the voice of God speaking out of the midst of the fire, as thou hast heard, and live? . . . Out of heaven he made thee to hear his voice, that he might instruct thee; and upon earth he showed thee his great fire and thou heardest his words out of the midst of the fire.

(Deut. iv. 31, 33, 36.)

Rabbinic tradition had elaborated this in at least one detail. The voice proceeding from the mouth of God divided into seven voices, and then into seventy tongues, that *all* peoples of the earth might hear and understand, each in their own language.

Admittedly this is Rabbinic midrash of uncertain date. But whether St Luke has it in mind or not he takes the same deliberate backward look to the supreme moment of Israel's sacred past because the heart of the New Testament gospel which he is recording is that with the coming of Christ the final meaning of that past has been realized and fulfilled. The promised reign of God had been envisaged by Jeremiah as a new covenant, an entirely new order of things wherein God will be our God in a new and unprecedented way for ever (Jer. xxxi. 31); it had been foreseen and described in Ezekiel's vision of the dry bones as quickening, life-giving Spirit (Ezek. xxxvii. 1 – 14). St Luke is here saying that this dreamed-of Age-to-Come is present fact. The activity of God's spirit is proof of its presence. The first Christians, Gentiles as well as Jews, were aware that they stood under the judgment and mercy of a *new* Law, the law of Christ: of dying and rising with him and living a new life in him; of undergoing a new exodus with him, and of being incorporated into a new Israel, the Church of his Body, the community of the Holy Spirit. It is the second of the two great meanings of Pentecost.

To sum this up: for prophets and kings who had long desired and waited for the consolation of Israel,[1] it had been axiomatic that the Age-to-Come would have a twofold uniqueness and glory: it would be the age of the Spirit; and it would be the age when the sacred Law (Torah) would verily come into its own. The New Testament proclaims that the Age-to-Come is come, in

[1] Luke x. 24.

this its expected twofold manifestation. The long-awaited kingdom is now realized in present experience as Spirit and as Law, the Spirit of Christ and the Law of Christ.

Most fittingly, it is a Hebrew of the Hebrews, St Paul, who contrasts for us the Old Covenant and the New. He claims that through his ministry Christ has been written on the hearts of his fellow-Christians at Corinth just as through Moses the Law was once written for Israel on tables of stone (II Cor. iii. 3). And this Law of Christ is also the law of the Spirit since, for St Paul, the risen Christ and the Spirit are virtually identified. 'The Lord is that Spirit' (II Cor. iii. 17). Through the Spirit, Christ dwells in the hearts of Christians. The law within them is Christ within them. The indwelling Christ has replaced the older Torah written at Sinai on tables of stone. For St Paul, that is, the true conditions for the New Age are already established because Spirit and Torah thus coincide: the future kingdom is already a present reality.

Multae terricolis linguae, coelestibus una (on earth many tongues; in heaven one). The story of Pentecost, the backward look of the Church to Babel and Sinai, is at the same time its forward look to the final consummation in heaven. As we saw in our first chapter, the Christian philosophy of history is an eschatology. The redeemed society, already realized within history, is nevertheless not yet what it is to be beyond history. In this hope we were saved.[1] Christ in us is the hope of glory.[2] This hope belongs to the Church, and to the individual in his place within the communion of saints. Its content is the glory of God.[3] Creation is to reach its goal in the purpose of God, when all things are to be summed up in Christ,[4] the image and glory of God in whom they were created; and Man is to attain his 'chief end ... to glorify God and to enjoy him for ever'.[5]

[1] Rom. viii. 24.
[2] Col. i. 27.
[3] Rom. v. 2.
[4] Eph. i. 10.
[5] *The Shorter Catechism of the Westminster Assembly* (1643), Answer to Question (1), based on Ps. lxxiii. 25 – 6.

CHAPTER VII

BAPTISM AND EUCHARIST

It is notorious that the sacraments provoke controversy, not only between the divided Confessions of Christendom, but also within each of those Confessions. Informed debate turns on the nature and operation of sacraments: they involve ritual action which is symbolic action: how is that symbolism to be understood? The use of water in Baptism, and of bread and wine in the Eucharist: are these *signs*, and no more; that is, visible words or acted metaphors which point beyond themselves and thus express what cannot be stated in words? Or are they *instruments* by which something in past time is made effectively present; that is, are they more than dramatic representations of religious truth, in that they convey and effect what they signify, and therefore in some sense *are* what they signify? Do they commemorate the sacrifice of Christ, or realize it? 'Significando causant' (by signifying they cause): what, precisely, does this mean at Font or Holy Table?

To put this concretely: in what sense is the water of baptism a 'bath of regeneration'? What is the exact relation of the Bread and Wine to the Body broken and the Blood shed on Calvary? What does it mean to say with St Paul 'buried with him in baptism' (Col. ii. 12) or 'ye do show the Lord's death' (I Cor. xi. 26)?

In all Confessions these questions evoke varying answers, which nevertheless do not differ greatly from one another in the last analysis. The issue between Pope Nicholas II and Berengar; or between the Lutheran *est* and the Zwinglian *significat*; or between Pusey and Maurice on baptism; or between protagonists and opponents of 'Devotions' in modern Anglicanism, involves differences of credal emphasis rather than of credal content, in spite of appearances to the contrary.

To attempt to discuss the subtleties of such issues within the limits of a single chapter would be as absurd as trying to write the history of England on a postcard. I propose, therefore, to consider the main issue by beginning with one illustration of it: one of the many provided by the long history of the Church.

I

Who knows what it means to say 'God'? He is beyond body, spirit and all that man can see, hear or think. . . . His power cannot be determined or measured since it is beyond comprehension. . . . It is outside and above all that is or can be, yet present and active everywhere, even in the tiniest leaf. . . . He himself is there, in every single creature, innermost and uttermost, around and about, through and through, within and without, behind and before. . . . Nothing is so small, yet God is smaller; nothing is so vast or so minute in extension, God is still more vast and more minute. Nothing that man can name or think can express the being and activity of him who is at once everywhere and nowhere.[1]

No informed Christian will find pantheism in these statements, even though Luther writes '*Gottheit*' instead of '*Gott*' in some of them. For Luther never fails to answer the question which such statements provoke: namely, how is this God to be concretely apprehended and known? The very dynamism of his confession of the divine 'aseity' takes him to the fundamental problem of revelation.

That God is there (*da*), and that he is there for thee (*dir da*), are two different things. He is there for thee when he adds his Word thereto and says, Here thou must find me. . . . Though he is everywhere in all creatures, and could be found in stone, fire, water or rope . . . it is not his will that I should seek him there without his Word, throwing myself into fire or water, or hanging by the rope. It is not his will that thou shouldest grope and fumble for him in any and every place, for he has ordained a certain way wherein men are to find him: namely, his Word.[2]

This means that for Luther, as for Christian theology of all periods and confessions, the whole process of man's salvation rests on the divine *exire* (outgoing). The basis of Reformation theology is the Word whereby God in his transcendent and omnipresent otherness deals actively and personally with men, here

---

[1] W XXIII, 137, 133; XXV, 135; XXVI, 339. I take these references to Luther's doctrine of God as 'alles seiende und doch nicht da seiende' from Erich Seeberg: *Luthers Theologie, Motive und Ideen, I. Die Gottesanschauung* (Göttingen, 1929), pp. 182 ff. (References to the Weimar edition of Luther's works are given as W.)

[2] W XXIII, 141, 151; XIX, 442.

and now, as their redeemer. Everything, said Luther, depends on the Word (*es liegt alles am Wort*).[1] The scriptural meaning and content of this Word is that 'Christ the Son of God is our Saviour.'[2] The Word is actualized for us men in the Incarnation. '*Christus ist Gott selbst*.'[3] In the Child in the manger, the Man on the cross and the Sacrament of the altar, God the Redeemer is personally and essentially (*wesentlich*) present. The redemption won for us, once for all, on the cross becomes '*efficax et potens*' in our hearts through the gospel sacraments. Baptism and Eucharist are sacraments of that redemption. Some modern Protestants are embarrassed, and most modern Catholics are surprised that Luther should have expressed himself constantly in terms such as these:

If I would have forgiveness of my sins I must not run to the cross, for there I do not find it yet dispensed to me. Nor must I strive to know the passion of Christ by an intense commemoration of it. But I must go *zum Sakrament oder Evangelio* (to the sacrament or gospel) where I find the Word which conveys, pours out, proffers and gives to me the forgiveness won on the cross.[4] ... Although the work of salvation was accomplished on the cross and the forgiveness of sins was won there, it cannot come to us otherwise than through the Word. The whole Gospel is incorporated in the sacrament by the Word.[5] ... For though Christ had been given and crucified for us a thousand times all were profitless if the Word of God came not to administer it and to bestow it upon me and to say, This is for thee.[6] ...

Now what is the sacrament of the altar? It is the true body and blood of our Lord Jesus Christ in and under the bread and wine, through Christ's word, appointed for us as Christians to eat and drink. And as we said when speaking of baptism that it is not mere water, so we may say again here that the sacrament is bread and wine, but not mere bread and wine such as is ordinarily placed before us at meals but bread and wine comprehended in God's Word and bound up in it. The Word, I say, is what makes and distinguishes the sacrament. ... It is certainly true that if the Word be omitted, or if the sacrament be regarded without the Word, we should have nothing but bread and wine; whereas if the Word remains where it should and must be, by means of it we have the veritable body and blood of Christ.[7]

[1] W XVIII, 204.
[2] W XXIII, 183.
[3] W XXIII, 141.
[4] W XVIII, 203.
[5] W XXX. I, 226.
[6] W XVIII, 202.
[7] W XXX. I, 225.

Kohlmeyer has argued[1] that Luther meant by *verbum* what the medieval theology of the Eucharist meant by *gratia infusa*. The Word corresponds to the infusion of grace in that it enters into the believer with all the power of God's promise: 'so shall my word be that goeth forth out of my mouth; it shall not return unto me void, but it shall accomplish that which I please, and it shall prosper in the thing whereto I sent it' (Isa. lv. 11). In short, the sacraments of the gospel are more than bare signs. The Word is not only dramatically represented at the font, or expressed in a figure at the holy table; it is actualized, because effectively expressed there. Sacraments are instruments, effective signs, of God's redeeming power.

A difference of emphasis in the theology of the Swiss reformer, Ulrich Zwingli, led to division within the reforming ranks. 'Sensuous objects', he wrote, 'are irrelevant in the life of the spirit. Faith, the sole requisite, needs no such external helps or assurances. Let a man lack faith and the whole Jordan poured over him will avail nothing.'[2] This argument, though typical of Zwingli's middle period only, as Walther Köhler has proved,[3] illustrates that tension which is found in all sacramental theology. All the reformers were agreed that there is no sacrament without faith (*nullum sacramentum sine fide*); and for Luther and Calvin, Zwingli's positive affirmation here is altogether right: it was what he denied here that they repudiated as a profane perversion of historic Christianity.[4]

Zwingli's positive principle, that religion is spiritual and inward, will never lack its witnesses. But he went further. He denied that God's grace requires external means for its communication to man; and that outward things of sense, such as water, bread and wine, are anything more than illustrative symbols when used in worship. Luther replied to this, of course, with what

---

[1] *Zeitschrift für KG*, XLVII (1928).

[2] *Commentarius de vera et falsa religione* (1525) in *Zwingli's Werke*, ed. Egli, Finsler and Köhler (1905 f.), III, 760.

[3] Walther Köhler, *Luther und Zwingli*, I (1924). Also *Das Religionsgespräch zu Marburg, 1529* (Tübingen, 1929), p. 34.

[4] So Calvin on Zwingli (CR XI, 438), 'quam profana sit de sacramentis doctrina'.

had been the witness of Christian theology from Romans i. 20 onwards: namely that 'what God does and effects in us he wills to do through outward means'.[1] This is common to all Christian Confessions. It was Calvin's constant witness that 'by these carnal elements he brings us to himself' (*nos ad se deducit*):[2] words which recall the classic sentence of Aquinas that it is the property of human nature to be brought (*deducatur*) to *spiritualia et intelligibilia* through *corporalia et sensibilia*.[3] Luther stated it thus:

For the spread of his holy Gospel he deals with us in twofold fashion; outwardly and inwardly. Outwardly he deals with us through the spoken Word of the Gospel and through material signs, namely Baptism and Sacrament. Inwardly he deals with us through the Holy Spirit and faith, along with other gifts: but in such measure and order that the outward element has to come first; the inward after and through the outward. God has so ordered it that he gives men the inward element only through the outward.[4]

Zwingli does not altogether repudiate this familiar sacramental principle, even in his more radical middle period. But whereas Luther understands the words 'Take, eat, this is my Body' with dogged realism, they are not more than a metaphor or figure for Zwingli. 'Is' means 'signifies'. Eating symbolizes faith in the Crucified (and therefore, we may add, comes very near to being its superfluous doublet). The Eucharist is a symbolic rite of commemoration and thanksgiving.

The constant pole by which Luther steers is the Real Presence. His treatise of 1523 on the adoration (*Anbeten*) of the Host attacks memorialist symbolism, and insists that 'he who believes that Christ's Body and Blood is there may not refuse reverence to it without sin. I am bound to believe that Christ is there'.[5] In a real, physical sense (*wahrhaftig und leiblich*) the communicant eats and takes to himself Christ's Body.[6] The words of institution unite the *res sacramenti* to the elements, and the Body and Blood is 'verily there' (*wahrhaftig da*).[7] It is hardly surprising that this

[1] W xxx. 1, 215.
[2] CR vi, 114; xxiii, 251. *Opera Selecta*, ed. Niesel, i, 118.
[3] *Summa Theologica*, Part III, Qu. 61, Art. i (conclusion).
[4] W xviii, 136.
[5] W xi, 417.
[6] W xxiii, 87.
[7] W xix, 489 – 90

provoked Zwingli's cry, 'Ah thou worthy Luther, God have mercy that thou hast uttered such a word; for it is thoroughly popish'.[1] Nor is it surprising that Zwingli regarded John vi. 63 (but *not* verses 53 – 6 presumably) as the most weighty utterance of Christ' (*gravissimus Christi sermo*), and as the 'iron bastion' of his position:[2] 'It is the spirit that quickeneth; the flesh profiteth nothing: the words that I speak unto you, they are spirit, and they are life.'

We must not pursue this particular issue further. I have used it to illustrate an abiding issue. It belongs to a chapter of Christian history which is closed in one generation only to be opened again in the next. We seem able to learn three things from it.

The first is that nature itself is a medium of revelation, a vehicle of the mystery of God's being. There is a true sense, as we must notice later, in which every Eucharist is a Harvest Festival. In principle, indeed, any object from among the common stock can point beyond itself to the infinite and the holy. 'Every type of reality', says Tillich, 'can become and has become a medium of revelation somewhere.'[3]

> . . . on some *gilded Cloud* or *flowre*
> My gazing soul would dwell an hour,
> And in those weaker glories spy
> Some shadows of eternity.

So Henry Vaughan. For Wordsworth it could be 'the meanest flower that blows'. The divine is disclosed through finite and common things as their transcendent meaning. It is the massively simple and common elements in nature which become our greatest religious metaphors: Bread, Wine, Water, Light, Rock, Wind, Fire, Darkness, Height, Depth, Blood, Dust, Oil, Rain, Lamb, Lion, Grass, Father, Son. These facts of nature and history are, at the same time, images; signs of spiritual meaning. Every page of Bible and Hymn-book attests this.

[1] Köhler, *op. cit.* p. 487.

[2] *Zwinglii Opera* (ed. Schuler and Schulthess), 1828 f., II, ii, 41 f.,; III, 257, 336, 339, 553, 606; IV, 53, 118.

[3] Tillich, *Sys. Theol.* I, 118.

But in the second place – and to adopt Professor Quick's distinction[1] – some of these signs are more than mere signs or symbolic pointers: they are also instruments. They have become bearers of power as well as meaning. This distinction between representation and instrumentality is one which has constantly been made in a variety of terms. So long as we do not unduly press the distinction we may summarize it thus. The function of the *signum* is pictorial, representative and even dramatic; it points to the divine. The function of the *signum efficax* is instrumental, operative and effective; it not only points to the divine, but participates in its active power. The one is a bearer of spiritual meaning: the other has become a vehicle of redeeming power. Dom Gregory Dix's witticisms about the 'real Absence'[2] in his criticism of the Anglican Reformers may remind us that he was there joining hands with Luther, who made the serious and acute observation in his *Table Talk* that 'philosophical and theological symbols are not synonymous: a *signum philosophicum* is a symbol of something which is *not* here (*nota absentis rei*), whereas a *signum theologicum* is a symbol of something which *is* here (*nota praesentis rei*)'.[3] And in his first formal and polemical treatise on the Eucharist, *That these words*, THIS IS MY BODY, *still stand firm* (1527), he makes the same point: 'The Eucharist is not a symbol of something absent or future (*eins abwesenden oder zukünfftigen dings*).'[4] It is instructive that the religious experience of devout Jews and Christians at Passover and Eucharist respectively almost always includes this sense of 'contemporaneity'.[5]

In the third place, the history of sacramental theology makes plain how short is the step to error which 'overthroweth the nature of a sacrament'. For it is the nature of a sacrament that the part of finite reality which is its *matter* is both asserted and negated at the same time. Its proper meaning is negated by the transcendent meaning which it mediates. Yet its transcendent meaning is

---

[1] *The Christian Sacraments* (Nisbet, 1932).
[2] *Church Quarterly Review*, June 1948.
[3] *Tischreden*, W IV, 666.
[4] W XXIII, 211.
[5] See p. 108 above and p. 145 below.

asserted only through the proper meaning which is the necessary basis of the mediation. Bread ceases to be bakehouse bread when the Bread of Life becomes its transcendent meaning: but the Bread of Life would cease to be the heavenly Food it is apart from the baker's loaf which mediates it. We may illustrate this from Marriage (which R. P. Casey[1] cites as the third of the four sacraments described by St Paul). Marriage is a union of man and woman for love of such supernatural quality and meaning that the closest analogy to it is the union between Christ and his Church. But that love is nevertheless through sex. Indeed, only through the 'secular' can the 'sacred' be expressed. The holy cannot appear save through that which is, in another aspect, secular. This is the meaning (or part of it) of Tillich's observation that religious symbols are double-edged.[2] They are directed towards the infinite and the finite at the same time. Any attempt to make infinite and finite mutually exclusive 'overthroweth the nature of a sacrament'.

II

It is clear that Christ himself is the perfect and supreme sacrament. All Christian sacraments derive from him, and are ministered by him; notably the four which were all-important for the man who is our earliest authority for the facts and beliefs on which our religion rests, namely St Paul.[3] For him Baptism, the Church, Eucharist and Marriage are an 'extension', in varying senses,' of the crucified and risen Christ, in that it is Christ who thus identifies humanity with his action, passion and victory in historic time. Baptism and Eucharist, in particular, make luminous and alive the redemption which God has brought to the human race in his Son. They are sometimes described as the two gospel sacraments, because behind them there is always the triumphant dying of the Lord Jesus.

The first thing to be noticed about the sacraments of our redemption is that *they mediate God's grace and make real to men its*

---

[1] R. P. Casey, 'Gnosis, Gnosticism and the New Testament', in *The Background of the New Testament and its Eschatology*, ed. W. D. Davies and D. Daube (Cambridge, 1955), p. 72.

[2] Tillich, *op. cit.* I, 240.

[3] R. P. Casey, *op. cit.* p. 72.

prevenient character. For the great and distinctive affirmation of the gospel of our redemption is not only that the Kingdom of God *has come* in Jesus the Christ, but that it has come as grace, without waiting for sinful men to deserve it or even to want it; it is the gift, out of sheer love, of him who has not waited for men even to repent. Grace is love in action, 'while we were yet sinners'. The clue to it is 'not that we loved God but that he loved us'. The teaching of Jesus, particularly in the parables, is a declaration that in the events actually happening before men's eyes through his ministry – acts of healing and works of mercy – the victorious reign of God is present reality; and that its character and meaning are, above all, redemptive. Here is loving-kindness going beyond all legal calculus of merit or demerit; here is grace, even for the unjust, the unthankful and the evil. It takes no account of fitness or desert; it 'refuses to be worn down or turned aside by any churlish refusal of it'.[1] In brief, it actively declares the redeeming love of God. Jesus made this amazing love credible by making it manifest. In his words of authority and deeds of power, and supremely in his sufferings and death, the Father's good pleasure to *give* the kingdom to his children is made plain for ever. The whole series of events from the Baptism in Jordan to the Crucifixion and the Resurrection, is one great act of God who has thus visited and redeemed his people.

God's *prevenient* grace means, then, that everything in the Christian religion depends on the divine initiative and gift. The Incarnation means that God so loved the world that he gave his only Son (John iii. 16). The Crucifixion means that God commends his love to us in that, while we were yet sinners, Christ died for us (Rom. v. 8). The Resurrection means that God giveth us the victory through our Lord Jesus Christ (I Cor. xv. 58). All is of God. Even our response to him in faith is his own gift. When we acknowledge our sonship and cry 'Father', it is the Spirit himself bearing witness with our spirit that we are the children of God (Rom. viii. 15 f.).

In short, the grace of God, as bodied forth in Jesus Christ, was

[1] C. H. Dodd. I cannot trace the reference.

in no way conditioned by the possibility that men might accept it, or by the probability that they would reject it. It was given, freely and fully. The final measure of the immeasurable gift was the loneliness and desolation of the total self-giving on Calvary. We have to remember that it was on the night when he was betrayed, and when he knew that even his devoted friends were about to deny and forsake him, that he *nevertheless* associated them completely with himself and gave to them the Bread of eternal life and the Cup of his new covenant. As during his ministry, so here at its climax, the kingdom of God is still an unqualified gift to undeserving men.

Baptism is the efficacious sign of this prevenient grace of God. It is more than a ritual fiction whereby dying with Christ and rising with him from the dead are dramatically illustrated by plunging naked beneath the water of baptism, and rising from it again to 'put on' Christ in newness of life. It is the actual means whereby the grace of the Lord Jesus Christ has been effectually and continuously communicated to believing men from the beginning, and whereby they have been verily *identified* with his death and resurrection. It is a symbol in the causative, efficacious sense of all biblical symbolism, in that it not only declares and illustrates God's grace in Christ, but achieves the purpose of that grace in and through the historic actuality of the Church of Christ's Body. It is the act whereby God himself incorporates the individual life of the Christian initiate into the corporate life of the risen Christ; and is primarily, therefore, something done with him and to him, rather than something which he does. The immense energies of the religious life are always rooted in a moment of complete human passivity wherein God acts. This is why the meaning of the baptismal act is expressed consistently by St Paul in the passive voice. 'Do you not know that all of us who *have been baptized* into Christ Jesus were baptized into his death? We *were buried* therefore with him, by baptism, into death, so that as Christ was raised from the dead by the glory of the Father, we too might walk in newness of life' (Rom. vi. 3 f.).

The New Testament does not allow us to forget, of course, that there is no sacrament without faith. In the effective sign of God's prevenient grace man's believing participation is already included. The necessary response of faith is itself God's gift. Throughout the story of the Acts the rite of baptism is explicitly associated with 'hearing the word' and 'believing' (see Acts ii. 37 – 8, 41; viii. 12 – 13, 35 – 6; xvi. 14 – 15, 31 – 3; xviii. 8; xix. 4 – 5). The evidence of the New Testament is explicit and inescapable that baptism presupposed faith, and would have been worse than meaningless without it.[1] This means that baptism was both objective and subjective in its reference. Grace and Faith – like 'outside' and 'inside', or like Luther's *Wort* and *Antwort* – are not separable in experience.

It was not the convert's faith as such, however, which made the plunge beneath the water an effective sign of the new age: the rite was *there* because the new age of which it was sign and seal was there: it had been there in all its givenness and potentiality ever since the baptism of the Lord himself in Jordan had announced and initiated the baptism of humanity by the Spirit; the coming of the kingdom of God. As Luther was to put it in his *Greater Catechism*, 'My faith does not make baptism, but receives it'.

III

And so we come to the notorious problem of infant baptism. The prevenient character of God's saving grace is nowhere declared so unambiguously as it is here. 'Infant' (*infans*) means 'not speaking': the word stands for human life at its least articulate; so incapable of responsible self-determination and conscious initiative that we even use the neuter pronoun to refer to 'it'. An infant of days cannot possibly seek God or respond to God with heart and mind. But its baptism is the efficacious sign that God has already sought it[2]; that Christ died for it; and that it is no stranger to the covenant of promise. We have seen that the

---

[1] The 'judgment theme' in the sacraments is unintelligible on any other basis. See C. F. D. Moule's essay on this subject in Davies and Daube, *op. cit.* pp. 464 – 81.

[2] Cf. Jer. i. 5.

prevenience of God's grace to man's faith is always the sequence
of Christian experience: that sequence is nowhere so dramatically
and completely asserted as at the baptismal font.

> Since, Lord, to Thee
> A narrow way and little gate
> Is all the passage; on my infancie
> Thou didst lay hold and antedate
> My faith in me.[1]

Why, then, is the practice of the overwhelming majority of
Christians throughout nineteen centuries a problem? Put shortly,
the answer is threefold. First, there is an uneasy and growing
awareness in modern Christendom that the virtually indiscri-
minate baptism of infants (largely because parents making no
real profession of the Christian faith, and having no intention of
so doing, nevertheless want to have their children 'done') is nothing less than a scandal: baptism thus becomes a demonic sign of the
teeming secularity of modern life. Second, even when the full
implications of infant baptism are recognized with proper seriousness by all concerned, the personal faith of the baptized, which all
New Testament accounts of baptism presuppose as necessary, is
here necessarily absent. Third, the world-wide denomination of
Baptists has long contended that the New Testament provides
evidence only for the baptism of *adults* who are *believers*; not for
the baptism of infants, a practice representing a type of thought
other than that of the New Testament, and which did not establish itself in the Church before the close of the second century.
Almost certainly wrong, on historical grounds, in what it denies,
this contention is far more right than wrong in what it affirms. In
any case, the problem it raises is real, and is no longer cavalierly
dismissed. Indeed, the debate initiated by the very important
witness of the anabaptists of the sixteenth century continues to-
day at the highest level, and is in the forefront of modern dogmatic
interest because of its urgent importance for practical and pastoral
theology. No less a figure than Karl Barth has entered the lists

---

[1] George Herbert, *Holy Baptisme*; quoted by W. A. Flemington, *The New Testament
Doctrine of Baptism* (S.P.C.K. 1948), p. 141.

to challenge the scriptural and theological soundness of infant baptism, and to say:

Neither by exegesis nor from the nature of the case can it be established that the baptized person can be merely a passive instrument (*Behandelter*). Rather it may be shown, by exegesis and from the nature of the case, that in this action the baptized is an active partner (*Handelnder*), and that at whatever stage of life he may be, plainly no *infans* (not-speaking) can be such a person.[1]

Certainly the New Testament provides no positive or explicit evidence for infant baptism. But this argument from silence could mean either that infant baptism did not then exist, or that it was so common as to be taken for granted. It would be surprising if the whole households reported as having been baptized in Acts xvi., 15, 31, 33; xviii., 8 and I Cor. i. 16, contained no children: yet none of these passages specifically mentions the baptism of a child. Cullmann's acute reply to this, however, is that there is no New Testament evidence for the adult baptism of sons and daughters born of Christian parents.[2] In short, the argument from silence proves nothing for either party to the controversy.

It is more important, because much more fruitful, to look at the environment of thought and usage in the ancient Jewish and non-Jewish world in which the forms of the Gospel first took shape; but to remove the spectacles of our modern Western individualism before doing so. For the solidarity of the family was the universal axiom of ancient thought, whereby children from their birth were regarded as sharing in their parents' religious status, objectively considered. 'The idea that a parent, especially the *paterfamilias*, should stand in a religious relation to God, merely as an individual, and distinct from his own flesh and blood, would never occur to the ancients, least of all to a Jew.'[3]

The New Testament evidence has to be seen against this background; or, rather, in this light. The Christian family or household was not conceived to be a collection of individuals, each deciding for himself his independent destiny. Its inner cohesion

[1] *The Teaching of the Church regarding Baptism*, tr. E.A. Payne (S.C.M., 1948), p. 41.
[2] *Baptism in the New Testament*, tr. J. K. S. Reid (S.C.M., 1950), p. 26.
[3] J. V. Bartlet, *Christian Baptism* (Free Church Fellowship Occasional Papers, v).

meant that an act of the parents so momentous as a change in their religious or covenant relation to God inevitably involved their children. It is precisely that organic unity which is presupposed by what St Paul says in I Corinthians vii. 14 about a mixed marriage: one Christian partner therein makes the other (heathen) partner 'holy'; and the children of the union are 'holy' from infancy for the same reason. Otherwise what is said in Ephesians vi. 1 f. would be unintelligible. For there children are bidden to obey their parents 'in the Lord'; which means that they rank as of the 'household of faith' and not as of 'those without'. The early Church believed in the imminent appearing (παρουσία) of the Lord, and it is hardly credible that, under the pressure of that conviction, Christian parents should not have wanted baptismal assurance that their children were included with them in the kingdom. That children were considered to be already within the gathered fellowship of the redeemed is clear from the Apostle's assumption that Christian motives are binding upon them. Their filial obligation is set in the context of the Christian community wherein they are fellow-members with their parents. From the first the conception of salvation is attached to the messianic *community*, and is corporate in its very essence (Acts ii. 39). 'The Lord added *to the Church* daily such as should be saved' (Acts ii. 47). As it is beyond controversy that the Church in the New Testament was made up of baptized persons, the New Testament knowing no gate of entrance to it save by baptism, the inference that infants were baptized into it seems logically irresistible.

The reference is further strengthened by the analogy between circumcision and infant baptism, which has been clear to the Christian Church from its beginning. St Paul explicitly states and interprets it in Colossians ii. 11f. And the instructive point is the Apostle's insistence on faith, as the essential element in each of these rites of initiation into the covenant community (Rom. iv. 11f.; Gal. iii. 6f.).[1] But in what sense was it essential? Circumcision was the seal set upon the *prior* faith of Abraham, the father of the circumcised, in the promises of God. Faith in those promises was

[1] Cf. Oscar Cullmann, *op. cit.* pp. 56 – 69.

likewise required from his descendants, and the same sealing rite of circumcision was given to them. But it was always given to them when they were infants, the faith which it sealed being their *subsequent* faith. Thus the close analogy between Jewish circumcision and Christian baptism is more than analogy; there is unbroken connection between them. The former is superseded by the latter by being completed and fulfilled, for it is administered to male and female (children?) alike, all being by baptism 'one in Christ Jesus' (Gal. iii. 28). Coming out of a religion in which children, through circumcision, had been made heirs of the promises which later they would affirm through faith, is it credible that the first Christians withheld from their children the sacramental seal of their new heritage in the promises now vouchsafed by God to the new Israel? As Tertullian was to put it, infants are thus 'designated for holiness and so for salvation' (designati sanctitati ac per hoc etiam saluti: *De Anima* XXXIX).

To sum up on this issue: two ideas were essential to the theory and practice of baptism in the early Church.

The first was the corporate idea of salvation in the messianic kingdom: a common life of divine grace and fellowship realized in the Body of Christ. In the early Church the energies of that life were seen to be real and powerful; and baptism was the initiating rite effecting the believer's incorporation within it. The Christian religion being thus essentially corporate in its reference, *infant* baptism was a logical extension of this fact.

The second was the idea of faith as inherently personal and individual: the Church, its proper home, was the 'household of faith'. It was a Body made up of members, each in vital union with Christ, the Head of the Body. The Christian religion being thus essentially individual in its reference, *believers'* baptism was the logical expression of this fact.

If this duality in the apostolic idea of the Church be lost, the apostolic practice of infant baptism goes wrong. For baptism, which *began* unquestionably with adults, originally meant the incorporation of individual, adult souls already quickened by faith in Christ; it denoted what public confession made obvious, a change from one way of life to a new way; it marked and gave effect to the believer's passage from a world in bondage to the glorious liberty of the children of God. This was the regulative idea of which infant baptism was the logical extension: it was the infant's birthright in the covenant of grace.

As long as infant baptism remained within this context of experience where it originated, it suffered little corruption, since it was properly understood, just as circumcision under the old covenant was properly understood. It declared proleptically the infant's full faith-relationship to God, in virtue of an actual relationship of 'nurture and admonition' by God's people in the household of faith.

But when infant baptism passed into another sphere of thought and influence, that of the Graeco-Roman world, it did not escape some corruption from quasi-magical and superstitious ideas. This 'lamentable retrogression'[1] began when attention became concentrated on baptism as regeneration; and when infant baptism began to be viewed as conferring, through its mere administration (*ex opere operato*), both forgiveness of sins and rebirth to newness of life. So bold a claim did sometimes correspond to psychological and moral realities in the first age of the Church, doubtless, because it did express facts of adult experience, confirmed and sealed in adult baptism. But now this began to be transferred to infant baptism by loose and dangerous analogy: dangerous, because an impersonal and automatic concept of sacramental grace dominated the pagan mystery religions. Their influence on the developing Church has been exaggerated, admittedly: but, in any case, an explanation of the changing theory and practice of infant baptism lies rather in the growing momentum of the doctrine of original sin. As my old teacher at Oxford, Dr J. V. Bartlet, put it:

Particularly as the Augustinian doctrine of total depravity through Adam spread, it made strongly for the baptism of all infants, out of mercy, lest they should die before receiving the regenerative gift of the Second Head of

[1] See G.W. H. Lampe, *The Seal of the Spirit* (Longmans, 1951), especially pp. 34, 53, 59 f.,
102 f., 115, 118 f., 130, 146 f., 149 f.

the race, to cancel the birth-inheritance of guilt from the first Adam. Thus it tended to set aside the primitive restriction to the children of believers, and thereby to rob the rite of its original meaning and to substitute for it another of a highly subjective order, viz. as a miracle wrought in and upon the infant's unconscious and undeveloped spiritual nature. Here, in this region of theological development, lies the real source of differences in modern baptismal theories and practices. In the intensity of their recoil from the baptismal regeneration of infants, Baptists have rejected infant baptism altogether.[1]

Infant baptism cannot properly flourish or truly exist save in living relation with a high concept of the Church, itself the result of a high experience of the Church as the sphere of Christ's unique rule and blessing. The event of Christian initiation is inseparable from the process of Christian nurture.

IV

Early in the history of music ground bass came into use. It was a short piece of bass repeated again and again, while varied harmonies were built over it in the upper parts. In the Mass in B minor, to cite a famous example, Bach used a very poignant ground bass descending chromatically, in the great Crucifixus.

The deep, poignant and triumphant ground to all the varied motifs in the theology of the sacraments is sacrifice. The drama which we announce or set forth in Baptism and in the Lord's Supper is a paschal drama. Indeed, the ground bass of the whole solemn music from Genesis to Revelation is the Lamb slain from the foundation of the world.

This is the supreme truth and meaning of the sacrament of the Lord's Supper or Eucharist. The deep and constant thought here is that of sacrifice: Christ's complete self-sacrifice and self-offering for the redemption of lost humanity.

The second great fact, then, about the sacraments of our redemption is that *they represent, 're-present' and so 'realize' the self-offering of Christ made once for all on the Cross*. The essence and heart of the Eucharist is more than commemoration in the so-called Zwinglian sense: it is, to quote Professor O. C. Quick, 'truly a sacrifice. For it is the externalization in human ritual of

[1] *Op. cit.* p. 29.

the self-offering of Christ which was once for all in fact externalized on Calvary'.[1]

The ritual *is* commemorative, of course. Remembrance is its vital basis. The classic liturgies of Christendom all begin with it (ἀνάμνησις.) What is 'realized' in the ritual action is something remembered, and unfailingly recited as such. For the redeeming action and passion thus 'perpetuated' is rooted in history; in what the Lord did and said on the night in which he was betrayed. He said, Do this in remembrance of me. The memorial action, in which the generations of men have engaged unceasingly ever since, is his own ordinance. Further, *our* remembering of this event of long ago is no fiction. In a real sense it is corporate, continuous memory. Not one Lord's Day has ever passed without this showing of the Lord's death by the Lord's people. That is, before ever a word of the New Testament was written, and years before the time when an account of what happened was handed on in writing by St Paul, believers were meeting at this Table. Our remembrance goes continuously back to the point in time when it was actual memory for those who had themselves been actual witnesses of the event. This unbroken, corporate memory is therefore living memory and living witness. History has been simply and acutely defined as 'what we remember'; and the Eucharist is primary and supreme testimony to a gospel which is no scheme of speculative idealism, and no 'cunningly devised fable'. The Gospel declares what the Redeemer did and suffered in historic time. We remember its happening.

As we have seen in previous chapters, the main clue to what we thus remember is eschatology. In the ministry of Jesus the future kingdom of God declares itself as a crisis of present experience, moving steadily to its climax. His teaching is not only verbal. He uses imagery and symbol: in particular, the traditional Jewish symbolism of the Messianic Banquet, the feast of the Age to Come, its Bread and Wine being the heavenly food by which man's life in God is ever sustained. The central meaning of his

[1] *Op. cit.* p. 198.

parable of the Great Feast is that this Banquet is already spread. 'Come, for all things are now ready.' And, like the prophets before him, the Lord reinforces words with symbolic action. On more than one occasion he gathers his followers, sometimes a great multitude, and distributes bread, after he has blessed it and broken it. These common meals mean that people (even the outcasts of society; Mark ii. 13 – 17) are here and now eating bread in the kingdom of God. Yet this table-fellowship is no copy of any existing institution, such as the *ḥābûrâh*: it is original and creative; for it always points forward to a climax of self-offering in death. Until the Lord can say of his work, from the very height of that climax, 'It is finished', men are not yet sharers, in the full sense, in the life of the kingdom which has come upon them.[1] This is apparent from the poignant sequence of sayings towards the end – especially those about the Cup – the 'ground bass' of which is offering and sacrifice for the recovery of a lost world. The Son of Man came 'to give his life a ransom for *all*' (πολλῶν being a semitism having the inclusive connotation of πάντων).[2] 'I have a baptism to be baptized with; and how am I straitened until it be accomplished'. 'For their sakes I dedicate (ἁγιάζω) myself.' 'Are ye able to drink of the cup that I shall drink of?' 'Father, if it be possible, let this cup pass . . . nevertheless, not what I will but what thou wilt.' 'Lo, I am come . . . to do thy will, O God.' 'It is finished.'

And so at the Last Supper, the last moment possible before the imminent death of the Host is to be accomplished, and his work finished – again there is symbolic action. It is *the* sacrament of the food in the heavenly kingdom. He took bread and blessed it, and brake it, and give it to his disciples: in like ritual manner he poured out for them a cup of wine. Through this sacramental action he

---

[1] Some of the substance of this paragraph is taken from the essays of T. W. Manson and C. H. Dodd in *Christian Worship: Studies in its History and Meaning*, by members of Mansfield College (Oxford, 1936), pp. 48 – 9; 73 – 4. The most comprehensive critical survey, known to me, of the large modern literature on eucharistic origins is Eduard Schweizer's long and valuable article 'Das Herrenmahl im Neuen Testament: ein Forschungsbericht', in the *Theologische Literaturzeitung*, October 1954, pp. 572 – 92.

[2] J. Jeremias, *The Eucharistic Words of Jesus* (Blackwell, 1955; second edition), pp. 124 – 5 give the linguistic evidence for this. Cf. I Tim. ii. 6.

was making them participators, beforehand, in the fulness of the kingdom of God which he alone embodied.

For there was still something more. It is the new, distinctive, decisive thing. The Lord added something to these familiar eschatological symbols of the Bread and the Cup. He said, 'This is my Body. .... This is the new covenant in my Blood'. In speaking thus he was already imparting to his disciples the reality, the benefits and the meaning of that sacrificial work which he was about to accomplish at the altar of the Cross. 'The kingdom of God is present in the person and the finished work of the Messiah. In him the life eternal is realized. In giving the Bread, therefore, he gives himself.'[1] The Bread was broken and the wine poured out within sight of, and virtually in the presence of his finished work, his broken Body and shed blood: and yet that work was, in actual fact, not yet finished. He is making his unworthy followers the sacramental partakers of that which, chronologically considered, is still to come – his death and resurrection. Here in these sacred, anticipatory actions and words he is associating and identifying them with his unique, redeeming sacrifice. This is why St Paul will be writing, a quarter of a century later, 'the cup of blessing which we bless, is it not the communion of the blood of Christ?'

Whether or not the formidable learning of Professor Joachim Jeremias of Göttingen, in the second edition of his book *The Eucharistic Words of Jesus*, has at last proved the strong case already presented by Dalman, Billerbeck and others for thinking that the Last Supper was the Lord's celebration of the Jewish Passover with his disciples, there is no doubt that the Supper was steeped in paschal ideas and associations. Whatever the date of the Crucifixion, Good Friday was too near in time to the day of the Passover to be interpreted without close reference to the ritual slaying, for each household or other group, of the Passover lamb. The redeeming death with which the Lord here identified his followers was the death of a sacrificial victim. In the ritual action of the

[1] C. H. Dodd, *op. cit. supra*, p. 74.

Supper he declares that he is about to die that death, making the broken bread and outpoured blood of the grape the acted parable and efficacious sign of the breaking of his body and the shedding of his blood. From the mysterious words *dēn bisri* (this my body) and *dēn idhmi* (this my blood) the command 'Do this' is plainly indissociable.

This fact has been the starting-point of unscriptural error and superstition, and of disastrous controversy and schism. Christians of all confessions have been slow to remember that Jesus Christ was, among other things, a poet and an artist: they have spent precious energies in fighting passionately over the dual problem of the exact relation of the real presence to the consecrated elements, and of the sacrifice once offered on Calvary to the eucharistic offering. Discerning minds are now asking from which of two abuses Christendom will turn out to have suffered more – the corrupt and superstitious use of the sacramental principle within Catholicism which inevitably provoked the Protestant protest: or the blind and continuous iconoclasm within Protestantism which has now come near to destroying the sacramental foundation of Christianity altogether, and therewith the religious basis of its own protest.[1] But in spite of this expense of spirit in a waste of shame in which every part of the Church universal has been guiltily involved, the *fact* of this great sacrament of the Body and Blood remains as the focal centre of all Christian worship and the deepest meaning of all Christian life. Only in our sacramental *identification* with the Redeemer's perfect sacrifice – the offering of himself in complete obedience even unto death – are we enabled to make that offering of ourselves to God in adoring gratitude and faithful obedience which is the initial and final meaning of the eucharistic sacrifice. The indissociable statement and command of the Words of Institution find their true and sufficient commentary in the indissociable statement and command of Philippians ii. 8 and Romans xii. 1.[2]

[1] See Tillich, *The Protestant Era* (Chicago, 1948), Introduction, pp. xxiii f.
[2] See the concluding paragraph of Chapter III above, p. 59.

V

The third great fact about the sacraments of our redemption, then, is that *they identify us with the Redeemer's Sacrifice and, by virtue of that identification, enable us to have fellowship with his sufferings and to dedicate ourselves to God as living sacrifice* (Rom. xii. 1). The Eucharist in particular, therefore, is supremely an act of corporate worship; it is holy, corporate communion of God's people with him and with one another.

Eucharist (εὐχαριστία) means thanksgiving as an act of worship. The word is applied in this sense by the oldest Christian liturgy we possess, the *Didache*, to its still older prayers. Its ninth chapter calls the rite *Eucharist* because prayers of thanksgiving are there prescribed to be said 'concerning the Cup' and 'concerning the Broken Bread'. This means that what consecrates the elements for their use as a means of Communion is, as it has been from the beginning, a prayer of thanks to God for all his gifts to man, in creation as well as in redemption. The post-communion prayer of the *Didache* contains the words: 'Thou, almighty Lord, didst create all things for thy name's sake. Thou didst give food and drink to men for their enjoyment, that they may give thanks unto thee, but to us thou hast granted spiritual food and drink and life eternal through thy servant.' It is our earliest liturgical illustration of the fact that 'in the early Church every Lord's Day was a Harvest Festival as well as an Easter Sunday'.[1] Indeed, we may quite legitimately and profitably remind ourselves how universal is this symbolism of communion which we have 'received of the Lord'. We need not, and may not, hesitate to recognize how close the Christian religion is here to the heart of all religion, including the most primitive. The Lord bids us eat and drink. Why does this constitute 'holy communion'? What does it mean? It means two things, as simple and universal as they are profound; for in this common act of eating and drinking is wrapped up the whole meaning of life.

[1] Prof. Alan Richardson, quoted by C. F. D. Moule, *The Sacrifice of Christ* (Hodder, 1956), p. 14.

(i) It means, first, our 'creaturely dependence'.[1] At every moment of our life from birth to death we depend, *absolutely*, on that which is not-ourselves. The self is distinguishable from the not-self only to be utterly dependent upon it. We survive and live only by what we receive from the great Reality beyond us. Each one of us, whether he be an Einstein or a pygmy in the Amazon jungle, is ever a humble pensioner at the gate of the Whole. We have bread because the grain of wheat falls into the ground and dies; we have wine because the grape yields its life-blood. All life involves this dependence on food; all food involves this sacrifice of life.[2]

The acknowledgment of this fact is the deep root of all religion. Its recognition in the sacred rites and ritual feasts established and observed by primitive peoples is of immemorial antiquity. Indeed, it is through these and similar rituals that men become aware of their communion with the power-not-themselves which gives 'spirit', as well as life, through the partaking of food. Their communion with the Corn-Spirit as they feed upon the corn is primitive men's way of saying 'the *Lord* hath visited his people, giving them bread': it is their awareness that Nature is ever the sacrament of *Spirit*.

We may observe in passing that it is just this universal aspect of religion which makes a testing contrast with the conscious sophistications of civilized culture. Discussing Stravinsky's *Le Sacre du Printemps* and *Les Noces*, W. J. Turner has drawn attention to

the curious fact that the subject-matter of both these ballets is an ancient ritual – in the one case the primitive rites of an agricultural people celebrating the mystery of sown corn rising from the earth again in the spring (which is embodied in the Greek myths of *Persephone* and *Adonis*); in the other case, *Les Noces*, the marriage rite as celebrated in a primitive society. Now what is interesting about these two works is that in each Stravinsky should have found it necessary to go back to the primitive myth. It is understandable that this should have been necessary in presenting the death and resurrection of the ear of corn. There seems to be no mystery in agriculture today. Those extremely inorganic objectivations of the will – the American harvesting machine, and the Dominion of Canada's offices in Trafalgar Square – shut out from ordinary

[1] C. H. Dodd, *op. cit.* p. 80.
[2] Cf. O. Fricke, *Die Sakramente in der Protestantischen Kirche*, p. 25: 'alle Nahrung ist geopfertes Leben.'

men's eyes the strangeness of what is happening behind them. But it might have been thought that a modern wedding was still sufficient of a mystery to have served Stravinsky's purpose. It would be an illusion to think so. . . . To discover anything sublime in the Canadian Government offices, or in a marriage at St George's, Hanover Square, would seem an impossible task for a genuine artist . . . Stravinsky, being a real artist, and therefore having some imaginative conception of the profound and extraordinary nature of the reality underlying these appearances, was forced to go back to the primitive forms in order to recover the sublimity which rightly belong to them. . . .[1]

Paganism itself is thus a rebuke to modern man. The protest in Stravinsky's music is, like Wordsworth's, a *religious* protest against the *in*dependence which is virtual godlessness.

> . . . Great God! I'd rather be
> A Pagan suckled in a creed outworn;
> So might I, standing on this pleasant lea,
> Have glimpses that would make me less forlorn:
> Have sight of Proteus rising from the sea;
> Or hear old Triton blow his wreathed horn.

It is Alice Meynell's protest, in her two verses entitled 'The Fugitive'. Some French publicist had written, 'We have driven away this Jesus Christ' (nous avons chassé ce Jésus-Christ); and she wrote

> Yes, from the ingrate heart, the street
> Of garrulous tongue, the warm retreat
> Within the village and the town;
> Not from the lands where ripen brown
> A thousand thousand hills of wheat;
>
> Not from the long Burgundian line,
> The Southward, sunward range of vine.
> Hunted He never will escape
> The flesh, the blood, the sheaf, the grape
> That feed His man, – the bread, the wine.

We need not hesitate to observe, then, that Christ employs this same symbolism. As dependent creatures we are to show our dependence by taking into our bodies that which is provided for us by 'the Power-not-ourselves'; such ordinary, vital things as bread and wine. For it is in Christianity, at the focal centre of its

[1] W. J. Turner, *Beethoven: The Search for Reality* (Benn, 1927), p. 325.

worship and life, that this our creaturely dependence receives its pure and true expression. It tells us here that the only power which thus imparts to us life in its fulness – life physical, spiritual and eternal – is the God and Father of our Lord Jesus Christ. The only Bread that nourishes and sustains us is the Bread which comes down from heaven (John vi. 32 – 5). As John Gerhard wrote of the mystery of Christ's Incarnation, he is laid in a manger because he is the true food of our souls. And of this holy food the Lord has said, This is my Body. Divine, eternal life comes to us in and through him. We do not think here in the vague terms of Matthew Arnold's mysterious 'Power-not-ourselves making for righteousness': we know the God and Father of the Lord who gave his life for us; who ever gives himself, and thereby gives us eternal life.

(ii) But this common act of eating and drinking means a second thing here. We do it together. This feast of holy communion with him who made us and on whom we ever depend means that we may receive his gift only by sharing it. Universal fellowship is the correlative of universal dependence. As we have noticed all along the Church is meaningless if this be not its ultimate meaning. We share with one another the life which we derive from God. Nor is this an optional matter for those who may feel so disposed. We *are* one body, because we all eat of the same bread. There is no getting over the strange fact of the commingling of organic elements in that bread and wine with my living substance, so that I am after all 'of one substance' (ὁμοούσιος) with the springing grass of the earth; and since you, too, are by the same metabolism nourished in the same way, our apparent separateness – our seemingly sovereign isolation from one another – is a half-truth only: our creaturely dependence is at the same time our creaturely interdependence. It is more than interesting that in our earliest explicit historical account of the Eucharist, that of Justin Martyr A.D. 140, the vital paragraph speaks of eucharisted food (εὐχαριστηθεῖσαν τροφήν) and of metabolism (μεταβολήν):

This Food is called by us Eucharist. . . . We do not receive it as ordinary bread and ordinary drink; but just as, by being made flesh through God's command, Jesus Christ our Saviour took both flesh and blood for our salvation, so also the food which is eucharisted through the words of institution, and from which our own blood and flesh are nourished by metabolism, is both flesh and blood of that incarnate Jesus.[1]

He says 'we' throughout, because this is no individual gift. We receive this gift of life – from nature, from history and from the eternal kingdom of God – only as we share it with one another. 'This is for *thee*', wrote Luther:[2] but he also wrote that we are 'one cake', 'one lump'. It is the primitive witness of the *Didache*, where the Eucharist for the Broken Bread says, 'As this broken bread was scattered (as corn) over the mountains, and being gathered together became one, so may thy church be gathered together from the ends of the earth into thy kingdom'. Eucharist, like Harvest, speaks not only of the physical necessities of man's being but also of his necessities as a social being. He who depends absolutely on the wholly-other, depends also on his fellows. Their communion with him is also a condition of his existence and his survival; nor can he have true communion with God apart from them. A Meal, then, is always more than the partaking of bread: it is a common partaking by those who, as members one of another, are one body.

Professor Dodd has observed that in I Corinthians xii. 27, Romans xii. 5, Ephesians iv. 12 and v. 30, St Paul 'pointed to an original and suggestive' interpretation of This is My Body. And the great imagery of Vine and Branches in the Fourth Gospel, like the thought of St Paul, belongs to the same eucharistic sequence: (i) we live by the life of God; (ii) the Bread is that life; (iii) we all partake of the same bread; (iv) Christ's Body is constituted by those who share with one another the divine gift of life which they share in and through him; (v) the Church is the Body of Christ, the communion of saints in history and beyond history.

The great and familiar theme which I have tried to develop may be summarized thus:

---

[1] Justin Martyr, *Apology* I, §66. The sentence is cumbrous and I have accurately paraphrased it, rather than literally translated it, at one or two points.

[2] See p. 120 above.

(i) THE MEANING OF NATURE

Nature is the vehicle of supernatural meaning and power. An object, event or action is sacramental when the transcendent is conveyed and perceived through it. *Nature is thus the sacrament of Spirit.*

(ii) THE MEANING OF THE BODY

The human body is rooted in nature and is a part of nature. Man's self-transcending being is there incarnate. His body depends absolutely on food and drink. But the human body is the highest creation of nature, in that here all the processes of nature are concentrated. They are concentrated in such a way that they transcend their lower forms and rise to the new level of freedom. This means that in the human body nature enters history; nature is here the supreme theatre of history. *The body is thus the sacrament of history.*

(iii) THE MEANING OF THE BODY OF CHRIST

In the life of the incarnate Christ the kingdom of God enters history. One of the great signs of its presence and power (as Tillich has constantly urged) is the healing of the human body. This means that in the Body of Christ nature reaches its fulfilment in history's centre; his Body is the perfect organ and experience of the Spirit. *The Body of Christ is thus the sacrament of the kingdom of God.*

(iv) THE MEANING OF THE EUCHARIST

The historic Body of Christ is obviously inaccessible to us. But bread and wine, which represent the forces nourishing and supporting the basis of man's highest spiritual possibility, here mediate to us Christ's divine gift of our total healing and redemption unto life eternal. We accept with adoring gratitude what God gives to us in him, and become (by the metabolism of his Body) what he makes of us. *The Eucharist is thus the sacrament of his Sacrifice and his Resurrection.*

VI

Anyone who knows anything about sacramental religion knows that to be thus confronted by the saving act of God in its intrinsic uniqueness is to be taken beyond temporal limitations. Those who have wrestled with the inescapable paradoxes of theology through the generations have always been at pains to say that in the Eucharist the Christian has a real experience (which he feels to be ontologically distinct from a vivid memory) of what once took place; that is, of what is now taking place again. Because Giver and Gift are here identical, without the Giver there would be no Gift. And the Giver is the eternal God, whose kingdom is neither past, present nor future in the human sense of those tense-distinctions: it *is* eternally. God being *totum simul* (All always, *or* the All, at once), human thought struggles to express divine simultaneity in terms of 'contemporaneity'.[1]

The research of modern anthropology into the ways in which so-called primitive peoples think may help us here. Their mentality being synthetic rather than analytical, they think in terms of relatedness; for them, perceived phenomena participate in some sort of whole; their thought 'grasps a totality', and this awareness of totality informs their sense of time and its passage. This may not be patronizingly dismissed as pre-logical and primitive. It recalls profound Semitic ways of thinking and of awareness. Every believing Jew understood this wholeness of time, supremely during the eating of the Passover meal. There, present and past tenses became indistinguishable. He was truly an Israelite only as he appropriated to himself those great moments in the history of Israel which disclosed the mighty acts of God. Because the exodus from Egypt was Israel's exodus, he was there; he took this fusion of past and present tenses (as Western man would express it) with realistic seriousness. He was there, too, at Sinai for the giving of the sacred Torah: indeed, his daily meditative study of the Torah was truly effective only as he could say, 'this day I myself have received this holy law from Sinai'. And so, at the annual Passover ritual, with its paschal lamb and unleavened bread, its bitter herbs and solemn recital of God's mightiest of his mighty acts of deliverance, he knew *himself* to have been redeemed from bondage in Egypt. Further, he looked forward as well as backward; here, too, the tense-distinction of the West was dissolved. Just as this present feast was a ritual realization of the historic past, so too it realized proleptically the future feast of joy in the messianic kingdom. Future as well as past become contemporary in the religiously apprehended 'now'.

Every believing Christian understands this. What is the Christian Year but a time-sacrament, conveying what it symbolizes through the temporal sequence of its festivals – Advent and Christmas, Epiphany and Lent, Holy Week and Good Friday,

[1] See p. 108 above.

Easter and Pentecost? It is the story of our race understood religiously and redemptively through that gospel story which is itself set in the context of *Heilsgeschichte* beginning in Eden and ending in the New Jerusalem. Certain historic events thus become perpetually contemporary in Christian worship. For, in Christian worship supremely, present tenses become past, and past tenses present. The Church means what it says when it declares 'Christ the Lord *is* risen to-day'; or 'This *is* the night in which thou didst first lead our fathers . . . out of Egypt'; or, when it asks, 'When they crucified my Lord, *were* you there?'

In his *History and the Gospel* and *The Parables of the Kingdom* (to name only these), Professor Dodd has reminded us that in proclaiming the gospel from pulpit, altar and baptismal font, the Church is the sacramental instrument for this making-present of divine action in historic time. God's 'mighty acts' of redemption in history are actually mediated and conveyed by every proclamation of the gospel to-day. The *kerugma* is the representation 'of those temporal events in which the kingdom of God came'. Real preaching of the Word places those who hear and receive it in the very presence, the *real presence*, of 'that eschatological event in which the Church had its origin'. If I understand this great modern interpreter of the New Testament rightly, the supreme importance of the sacraments lies in their contemporaneity. In the Eucharist, the Church is neither *simply* recalling a last supper in an upper room long ago nor *simply* waiting expectantly for the banquet of the redeemed in the eternal kingdom at history's 'end': it is experiencing *now* the *geminus adventus Christi*; his coming in humiliation and his coming in glory.

In its rediscovery of man as *animal symbolicum* modern thought is learning from depth-psychology (the racial subconscious being the great symbol-creating source) what art has always known namely that the sense of contemporaneity is expressed through symbol rather than in ideas ground out by the clumsy machinery of the intellect. It is the art of a Dante, a Raphael or a Blake which can, in Donne's splendid phrase, 'contract the immensities'; and it is Hebraic-Christian rite and liturgy, rather than the wordy abstractions of conceptual analysis, which convey the 'telescoping of time'.

Some years ago the French artist Bérand depicted Christ at the house of the Pharisee with all the figures in modern evening dress. In this there was nothing new. To illustrate the Christian Year many an old engraving uses the age-old technique of showing several *successive* episodes all occurring simultaneously in various parts of the picture. And now Stanley Spencer's work asserts the same existential meaning of the gospel story. The Baptism is seen in a crowded municipal swimming-pool on the Thames. The Crucifixion takes place in the centre of Cookham High Street just outside *The Kings Arms*, and those who drive the nails wear the caps and tassels of brewer's draymen. To Spencer, the teaching of Jesus is more than a theme for analysis in the latest valuable monograph published by the Student Christian Movement Press: it is Christ preaching at Cookham Regatta in a black straw hat. Only in the 'now' of revelation and decision are the alpha and omega of history fused into unity. Having the loins girt and the lamp lit means living *now* in the dimension of the eternal which disclosed itself once for all in the fulness of time.

CHAPTER VIII

THE BODY OF CHRIST AND RESURRECTION

A youth went up to Oxford in the seventeenth century and applied for admission to Magdalen College. He was ushered into a chamber hung with black and lit by a single taper. When the president of the college appeared – a gloomy Puritan with nine nightcaps on his head – the boy's examination related not to Latin and Greek as he had expected, but to personal religion; and the interview reached its climax with the question whether he was prepared for death. Whereupon he fled, never to return.

That, at least, is Addison's story,[1] his urbane caricature of Puritanism in Cromwell's England. Caricature, however, is never mere invention. To be effective it has to exaggerate known and recognized facts. And the indubitable fact which this caricature recalls is that the Puritans took a solemn view of death because they took a solemn view of life. Were they morbid in so doing? We may grant that to be serious is a heavenly grace and to be solemn is a nasty sin; but is it unhealthy to insist that making sense of life must mean making sense of death? Can anyone live 'as ever in the great taskmaster's eye' and ignore the issue?

The issue is not peculiar to Puritanism, of course. Philip of Macedon had a slave to whom he gave a standing order. The boy had to enter the royal presence every morning, no matter what the king was doing, and to say to him in a loud voice, 'Philip, remember that thou must die'.

That was over two thousand years ago but, like Puritanism, it refuses to be dated. Man's preoccupation with his mortality is universal. It is Everyman's ultimate anxiety. Attempts to reason it away are futile. Death is the doom of all living things, and in this final humiliation man, too, is laid low with animals and plants.

---

[1] *The Spectator*, no. 494.

it is the inevitable and only outcome of every human life – inscrutable, unanalysable, unrehearsable, final. In a famous essay Bacon therefore made the cool observation that it is as natural to die as to be born.

But is it? Why then does death distress us; and why is the problem of death the deepest which human nature knows, and the fear of death the ultimate fear from which all other fears derive their power? The Christian faith gives two reasons why.

I

In the first place, man cannot away with the feeling that his death is unnatural as well as natural. 'He thinks he was not made to die.' Something in his deepest being rebels at death, not only the death of the young cut off in their prime but also the death of the old, whose individuality and wisdom are irreplaceable. Tillich has acutely observed that we rebel at the sight of a corpse.[1] Cynicism may dismiss this as familiar human conceit, but man has not been able to believe that his finite and transitory life in time gives an exhaustive account of what he is. The Christian faith has never forgotten what it learned from its 'old loving nurse, the Platonick philosophy', that men are aware of time because they belong to eternity. Our very consciousness of clock-time, of temporal succession and change, is possible to us only because God has set eternity in our hearts. It is only because we are made in the image of the Eternal that we speak of 'this bank and shoal of time' at all. Like the animals we are creatures of time and sense; but, unlike them, we know it. And it is because we thus transcend time that we do what ape or eagle or termite ant cannot do: we look before and after, and carry the tragic knowledge of our temporality; we keep our clocks wound and consult our calendars. In the very act of calling ourselves mortal we presuppose the immortal and the eternal; the absolute is already implicit in the relative; our finiteness has meaning only in correlation with infinity. It is arguable, indeed, that genuine finiteness belongs to man alone, since he alone is able to look beyond it. It is his power

[1] *The Shaking of the Foundations* (Scribner's, 1948), p. 70.

of transcending his finitude which alone makes possible his awareness of his finitude.

That little beaver up in the Canadian forest, building his dam of brushwood in the icy water, – is he aware of time? According to the animal psychologists there is some mental process in him whereby he can say to himself (as it were), 'It is snowing'. But in the shimmering heat of July he does not say to himself, 'It is not snowing to-day'. Locke's 'general ideas' are not for him.[1] To-day and yesterday are not for him. He is not consciously concerned with to-morrow even though he builds by instinct for it. Only man is genuinely concerned with to-morrow, and the irrevocable yesterday, and the pathos of his mortality. Only a Macbeth can brood over time as the way to dusty death. Death is the common doom, admittedly, of this Macbeth and this little beaver; of elephant and chimpanzee and the most intelligent sheep-dog that ever was. But Macbeth is aware of it as they can never be. They die; he *has* to die. There is a difference of dimension between dying and having to die; and in this very difference – in this distinctively human awareness of a temporality which expresses itself supremely in death – man already stands above temporality and death. He is aware of time because he belongs to eternity.[2]

Thus, man's death is not just 'natural' – and that's that. It involves an incomprehensible contradiction. A man's life, which finds its meaning only in eternity, is nevertheless without meaning because it ends in a grave. And the whole human story in all its glittering multiplicity comes at last to the same, empty, senseless, nothingness. Every column in the cosmic account adds up to precisely the same result, zero. In this tragic contradiction the old problem of physical evil reaches its climax.

So much for the first reason. The Christian faith goes further because it is also concerned with the old problem of moral evil.

[1] *Essay Concerning Human Understanding*, II, ii, 10: 'The having of general ideas is that which puts a perfect distinction betwixt men and brutes, and is an excellency which the faculties of brutes do by no means attain to.'

[2] Cf. J. L. Stocks, *Time, Cause and Eternity* (Macmillan, 1938), p. 143: 'The perception of temporal succession itself proves that the perceiver is in some respect other than temporally successive, which is to say that the perceiver has in some respect non-temporal or timeless being.'

There is a second reason for human distress here. Death supremely illustrates not only man's bondage to time, but also his bondage to sin. It is the moral conscience which makes our consciousness of finiteness so poignant. 'Out, out brief candle' is more than pathetic; it is appalling, because the guilt of Lady Macbeth so interprets it: 'Out, damned spot, out I say. All the perfumes of Arabia will not sweeten this little hand.' Exactly. St Paul clinches it in six words: 'The sting of death is sin.'

Sin is not a tiresome Puritan bogy. And it is more than merely missing the mark: our occasional failure to live up to our ideals, those splendid and flattering estimates of what we really are. The abominations and degradations of history are always with man; he does not outgrow them. This, the abiding human predicament, may not be dismissed with the facile advice

> If at first you don't succeed
> Try, try again.

Sin is man's refusal of his distinctive endowment and destiny as a child of God. It is his presumptuous and tragic attempt to be his own god; the proud and idolatrous worship of the self. In brief, it is rebellion and alienation. Man is not a son in his father's house but a prodigal in a far country. 'Your iniquities have separated between you and your God, and your sins have hid his face from you that he will not hear.'[1]

Thus something more than man's finiteness makes death his last enemy. His metaphysical distress is intensified by his moral distress. Death is our supreme anxiety not only because we have to die but also because we deserve to die.[2] Death marks man's last opportunity: because of his proneness to sin it ceaselessly threatens to mark a lost opportunity. It is therefore the living man's supreme crisis, his finally decisive choice. It is the crucial formulation of the question which is ever addressed to man; whether he will know God or not. The supreme issue of death is not whether we have a soul or, if so, whether it survives when the

---

[1] Isa. lix. 2; also i. 15

[2] Tillich, op. cit. p. 171.

body is buried or burned or drowned or blown to bits: it i
whether we will live with God, which is heaven; or withou
him, which is hell.

In short, death is sacramental. As the sacrament of time it is als
the sacrament of sin.[1] Just as a sacrament conveys what it sym
bolizes and in some sense *is* what it symbolizes, so death sym
bolizes and conveys the irrevocable actuality of sin as rebellior
against God and estrangement from God. As the supreme ex
ternal manifestation of our temporality it is also the suprem
actualization of our guilt. The carnal mind, says St Paul, is en
mity against God. Death defines that enmity with stark com
pleteness. It thereby defines man's deepest need as forgiveness anc
reconciliation. For a Christian, therefore, the distinctive conten
of immortality is not so much survival as salvation. Is there ;
faith which gives meaning and victory to our historical existenc
in spite of the meaninglessness and condemnation whereof deatl
is the *signum efficax*? To ask this question is to come to the greates
thought of which man is capable, the thought of God. May mai
hope to share in the eternity and the holiness of the divine life
Is God my saviour as well as my maker and judge?

II

The Christian faith meets sin and death not with the aspiration
of human idealism nor with the efforts of human legalism, bu
with the deed of God in Christ, the Everlasting Yea of the Gospel
It declares that we are justified, made right with God, not because
of anything meritorious that we have done, but because of some
thing which the eternal God himself has done in and through the
particularity of the time process: subjecting himself to transitori
ness and death and hell in the person and work of his Son, tha
he may save us unto life eternal. In the action and passion of the
man called Christ, God has conquered death's damning powe
over the creature called man. That is the Christian gospel. It
good news about immortality is the forgiveness of sins: it i
salvation through Jesus Christ, God in the flesh, crucified anc

[1] The phrase is James Denney's.

risen from the dead, and now alive for ever in the Church of his body, through the Spirit. The great and innumerable multitude of the redeemed, on earth and in heaven, *is* the Body of Christ.

And so we come to the supreme glory and mystery of the Christian revelation, the resurrection of Jesus Christ from the dead. The Gospels do not explain it: it alone explains them. We cannot begin to understand what happened when he 'rose from the dead': that is, *how* it happened. Our ultimate concern is not with the *how* of sheer miracle, alien to all our experience and inscrutable to all our enquiry; to be effectively real our concern is with its essential meaning. That meaning is at least threefold.

First, the Resurrection declares that Christ, the God-Man, was man in the most typical of all human experiences. Not only did he live our human life: he died the human death. Unlike Enoch who is translated, or Elijah who is taken up to heaven in a chariot of fire, he, the incarnate Son, is crucified, dead and buried. Buried in a grave is Israel's (and Everyman's) realistic symbol of the awful finality of death: what the Bible describes as being cut off from the land of the living.[1] Christ, then, was buried. This was essential to the Incarnation of God the Word. This was involved in his becoming Man. To be the Christ, God's dynamic self-disclosure as Judge and Redeemer, he had to be dead and buried.

Second, the Creed declares that he descended into hell. The tremendous words mean that in that Descent he was fulfilling the Incarnation to the uttermost. Not only did he die the death which we, as mortals, must all die; he also died the death which we, as sinners, must all die. To use that Pauline language which ought to shock us, he was 'made sin' for us. If St Paul stops short of saying that he was 'made guilt' for us,[2] the Creed is more explicit: 'He was crucified, dead and buried; he descended into hell.' The change there from the passive to the active voice has not lacked its commentators. 'Crucified, dead and buried': that is what men did to him. 'He descended into hell', that is what he did for men. The change from the passive to the active means that

---

[1] Isa. liii. 8.
[2] II Cor. v. 21. See p. 72 above.

he deliberately identified himself with us sinners, sharing of set purpose in our alienation and separation from God, albeit without sin. 'No man taketh my life from me, but I lay it down of myself.'[1] He chose that dread banishment from the bosom of the Father, the agony of separation from God at death, which calls across the centuries in the Cry of Dereliction: 'My God, my God, why hast thou forsaken me?' This, like his final commending of his spirit into the Father's hands, is integral and necessary to the christological paradox of his redeeming work: as Calvin dared to put it, 'He endured in his soul the dreadful anguish of a condemned and lost man'.[2] To put it otherwise, his Passion was representative; his endurance and deed were for the human race itself. He came to the fight and to the rescue as God's second Adam. As in Adam all died, even so in Christ all were to be made alive.

Third, only against this background of death and darkness is the Resurrection the Gospel of our salvation. The Gospel is good news because the victorious Redeemer has identified himself with sinning, suffering and dying men that they may thus share in his sacrifice and victory. He takes humanity itself with him through the valley of the shadow. We share, even now, in his victory. We have been sharing in it ever since our baptism. Where any man is 'in Christ' there is the new creation; the new exodus from bondage; the new covenant written in the heart; the new law; its fulfilment by the new man, within the fellowship of the new Israel which is the Church, the Body of Christ, itself the microcosm and proleptic realization of the kingdom of God, the final glory of redemption in a new heaven and a new earth. The clue to this comprehensive concept of re-creative newness is the act of God in Christ, which is reproduced and extended in those who believingly receive it. The New Testament does not shrink from the most realistic of metaphors to describe this identification of believers with Christ. Here is one: 'I am crucified with Christ. Nevertheless I am alive; and yet not I but Christ is alive in me: and the life which I now live under physical

[1] John x. 18.
[2] *Institutio,* II, xvi, 10.

conditions I live by the grace of the Son of God who loved me and gave himself for me.'[1]

III

But this New Testament metaphor of identification is misinterpreted if we fail to remember that its meaning is twofold. It has two complementary aspects, the individual and the corporate.

(i) The famous words just quoted from the Epistle to the Galatians illustrate the first of these two aspects: the individual believer is identified with Christ. 'Christ liveth in *me*.' St Paul put it thus in the first person singular because the evangelical experience of the saved soul is indefeasibly individual. We must notice in a moment that this emphasis is not the whole truth about being 'in Christ'; yet it is truth. We cannot get away from individuality merely because the twentieth century has rediscovered the error and danger of individualism. Whitehead's unfortunate dictum that religion is what a man does with his solitariness is, at any rate, a half *truth*: there is an obvious sense in which human personality is an ivory tower, inherently private and inviolable; its door is barred on the inside, and even the divine importunity will not force an entrance. 'Behold I stand at the door and knock.'[2] This sanctity of the individual is a dimension of personal being as God has made it. We have noticed in a previous chapter that man's moral structure is its correlative.[3] Moral responsibility presupposes individuality. The sense of guilt is the great guardian of our personal identity. Again, man's physical structure is its correlative: the sovereign isolation of his body within its fleshly integument involves the same inalienable individuality. We are born separately and we die separately. In Pascal's words '*on mourra seul*' (you will die alone). 'Every man', wrote Luther, 'must fight his own fight with death. . . . In that hour I may not stand with you, nor you with me.' That may not be discredited as typical 'Protestant individualism'. It will always be relevant because it will always be inescapable. Dying is the most private act that anyone

[1] Gal. ii. 20.
[2] Rev. iii. 20.
[3] See p. 103 above.

will ever perform. If, therefore, the resurrection life in Christ beyond death is to mean anything consonant with the life of time and sense this side of the grave it must at least include individuality in some form. God loves with an everlasting love not just humanity in general, but this John Doe, that Richard Roe, and their like, of whose separate individualities our multitudinous humanity is always made up. When St Paul writes 'he loved *me* and gave himself for *me*', the wonderful words mean precisely what they say. We need no more cogent reason for the high estimate of the individual person which has always been characteristic of the Christian faith.

(ii) But our identification with Christ has another aspect, the corporate and the cosmic. Even the mutual indwelling of Christ and the individual Christian asserted in Galatians ii. 20 was more than a private, spiritual experience, as St Paul himself repeatedly makes clear; it was inseparable from the unity of individual believers with one another in the one Christ (cf. John xvii. 20 – 1). The Hebrews had a strong sense of the corporate, and the apostle was a 'Hebrew of the Hebrews'; his doctrine of the Body was of vital importance for his theology. This has been worked out by Dr J. A. T. Robinson in *The Body: A Study in Pauline Theology*, a book which corrects a frequent misplacement of emphasis. He shows that the many phrases whereby St Paul extends the death of Christ to the dying of the individual mean what they say. They 'presuppose a nexus not of example but of something that can be expressed only by a variety of prepositions'. He lists a large number of these Pauline phrases which indicate quite unambiguously that it is *in*, *with* and *through* Christ's crucifixion and death that those who are *of* Christ 'have crucified the flesh with the passions and lusts thereof' (Gal. v. 24). Baptized *into* him they 'were baptized into his death' (Rom. vi. 3) and 'did put on Christ' (Gal. iii. 17). Dr Robinson then adds (the italics are his):

All these phrases depend for their understanding on a single assumption and mean nothing without it. It is the assumption that *Christians have died in, with and through the crucified body of the Lord* (have a share, that is, in the actual death that He died unto sin historically, 'once for all' (Romans vi. 10, R.V.M.))

because, and only because, they are now in and of His body in the 'life that He liveth unto God', viz., the body of the Church. It is only by baptism into Christ, that is 'into (the) one body' (I Corinthians xii. 13), only by an actual 'participation in the body of Christ' (I Corinthians x. 16, R.V.M.), that a man can be saved through His body on the Cross. The Christian, because he is in the Church and united with Him in the sacraments, is part of Christ's body so literally that all that happened in and through the body in the flesh can be repeated in and through him now. This connexion comes to clearest expression in Romans vii. 4: 'Wherefore my brethren, ye also were made dead to the law *through the body of Christ*; that ye should be joined to one another, even to him who was raised from the dead'. Here the words in italics mean *both* 'through the fact that Christ in his flesh-body died to the law' *and* 'through the fact that you now are joined to and are part of that body'. . . . The concept of the Body supplies the linch-pin of Paul's thought. . . . It is almost impossible to exaggerate the materialism and crudity of Paul's doctrine of the Church as literally now the resurrection *body* of Christ. The language of 'membership' of a body corporate has become so trite that the idea that the individual can be a 'member' has ceased to be offensive. The force of Paul's words can to-day perhaps be got only by paraphrasing: 'Ye are the body of Christ and severally membranes thereof' (I Cor. xii. 27).[1]

It must be admitted that this 'mysticism of Paul the Apostle', as Schweitzer called it, can be strange and baffling if pressed: to many it is therefore unpalatable and even repellent. Even for those who realize that individuality cannot be held to express the whole truth here, this exegesis raises difficulties. The case of incest within the Body (I Cor. v. 1 f.) is only one of many such difficulties. St Paul's emphasis on faith, and his dominant concern with moral realities, are reminders that the personal aspect of religion and ethics is of the essence of Judaism and Christianity. The apostolic preaching of the One Body has moral implications which only its individual members can honour. In his *One Body in Christ*[2] Dr Best argues that 'body' in St Paul's ecclesiology is not ontological but metaphorical, and that the clue to the right understanding of it lies in the Hebrew concept of corporate personality, vividly brought home to Saul, the persecutor of the Church of God, in the words 'why persecutest thou *me*?' Dr Best contends that St Paul's various figures, of which 'body' is the chief, are projections of the idea of corporate personality on the

[1] J. A. T. Robinson, *The Body* (S.C.M. 1953), pp. 46 – 7, 51.
[2] E. Best, *One Body in Christ* (S.P.C.K. 1954).

plane of metaphor, attempts to express this non-logical truth in logical categories. 'Body' is a figure for the structure, but not the work, of the Church. The Church is a fellowship, binding Christians to each other in their Lord: it is not an instrument of Christ's work in the world in the sense that it is an actual extension of the Incarnation and the Atonement, since Christ is sinless but the Church is not.

It is doubtless dangerous to assert *simpliciter* that the Church is an extension of the Incarnation. But Dr Robinson's discussion seems to me to be an important corrective of the Christian individualism which fails to take even the metaphor of the Body with full seriousness. In any case, a valid metaphor is what it is just because it has ontological implications; and it is beyond controversy that the full force of this great metaphor has to be included in what the first Christian man in history of whom we have any real and intimate knowledge[1] did understand by the gospel of Good Friday, Easter and Pentecost. Further, it was faith in this dimension and in no other which made Christendom. It assigned a new value and a high place to the individual, as we have seen: of necessity Christianity made its primary appeal to him, declaring him to be a new man in Christ, a new creation. But the new man is such only within the new community, the fellowship of the one body, the household of faith, the communion of saints. It has often been observed that though the New Testament refers to the Church as 'the saints' – those, that is, who are set apart – it never calls any one individual a saint. And Christ's apostles did not preach a message of spiritual self-training for individual sainthood, saying 'Follow Christ and so save your soul'. They called men to confess their estranging sin by acknowledging Christ as Lord and, then and there, to enter into the fellowship of the Church by the rite of baptism, wherein the old egocentric solidarity of men in sin and death would be changed into the new christocentric solidarity of the one body. Indeed, as we saw in the previous chapter, their language about the symbol of baptism

[1] 'Among all the great men of antiquity there is none, with the exception of Cicero, whom we may know so intimately as Saul of Tarsus' (W. R. Inge, *Outspoken Essays* (Longmans, 1919), p. 205).

was much more realistic than this. In the *locus classicus*, Romans vi (with its parallel in Colossians ii), the plunge beneath the water is a death and burial with Christ; and the emergence from the water is resurrection with him to newness of life.

To sum up here: identification with Christ can and must be expressed in terms of the individual as the great words of Galatians ii. 20 show. But the New Testament normally says 'we' rather than 'I'; its eschatology is not so much individual as corporate and cosmic, since this is the genius of Hebrew religion in contrast to that of Hellenism.

In our opening chapter it became clear that the Orphic-Platonist tradition of Hellenism is concerned with the vertical dimension of the eternal, rather than with the horizontal dimension of historic time. And so its eschatology, if the term be appropriate at all, is individual rather than cosmic. It conceives of redemption, not in terms of an end or goal of history (a concept unintelligible to the Greek mind) but in terms of the personal destiny of each individual at the hour of his death. The material, temporal order is destined to perish and is therefore irrelevant, save for its disciplinary function of bringing individual souls to redemption in the heavenly places. History may be an endlessly recurring cycle for all that this tradition knows; its only eschatology is one of individual escape from all that is implied by man's historic life in the body; *individual* deliverance from 'this muddy vesture of decay'.

Not so the Hebraic-Christian tradition of the New Testament. Here time is real and momentous because it actualizes the redemptive purpose of God in history, through history and beyond history. Here eschatology is cosmic and universal because it takes the whole process of history seriously. In the end the whole body of humanity will be God's people, and the whole created order will be re-created and transformed. For the New Testament gospel of the resurrection does not proclaim the redemption of individuals *from* the thraldom of time and history (as does Platonism in its various forms); it proclaims the redemption of the imperishable community of individuals *through* time and history. The focal centre of the worshipping life of God's people is the

communion of the body and blood of Christ. And this is what
the resurrection of the body ultimately means.

IV

But this gives us pause. For the resurrection of the body is a
biblical concept so inconceivable, baffling and even offensive to
modern man that, though he be a Christian, consciously or un-
consciously he puts something different in its place; namely the
non-biblical, Greek concept of the immortality of the soul which
illustrated our contrast between Platonism and biblical religion
in our first chapter, and has just now illustrated the related contrast
between individual and cosmic eschatology.

This contrast may still help us, for here again we may legitimately begin with the individual. If immortality means anything
that matters to us it must at least include the immortality of this
individual self and that – of Tom, Dick and Harry. But, let me
repeat, modern man is prone to interpret this in terms of the Greek
'immortality of the soul' rather than of the biblical 'resurrection
of the body' because the persistence of the individuality after
death as pure spirit seems more intelligible and more credible.

But is it? Niebuhr has reminded us that resurrection from the
dead, however conceived and expressed, lies beyond the limit of
the conceivable, since its necessary meaning is that our historical
existence is somehow consummated beyond history.[1] Is the
Greek concept of the immortality of the soul any more conceivable
than the biblical faith that the richness and variety of our life in
time will not be annulled in eternity and so lost for ever, but
lifted up into eternity and so fulfilled? Can we even begin to conceive of the soul as such; that is, immaterial and naked, artificially
separated from all relation with its vital context and environment?
The soul thus isolated is an abstraction: a life of Beethoven from
which everything to do with music had been eliminated would
be almost as meaningless.

Greek anthropology – and later idealistic thought which was
its legatee – presupposed a psychological dualism; the body was

---

[1] *The Nature and Destiny of Man* (Scribner's, 1943), II, 295.

a material instrument of which the soul made use; physical and psychical were clearly differentiated.

Hebraic anthropology, on the other hand, was pervaded by the sense of their indivisible oneness. Man's life in time is always bodily life; he knows no other kind of life. And it is part of the realism of scripture that it knows nothing of man as disembodied spirit. To quote Wheeler Robinson's now classic sentence: 'The Hebrew idea of personality is an animated body, not an incarnated soul.' In the Bible, then, there is little or no dualistic distinction between body and soul. Strictly considered, Hebrew language has no word for either. 'The body', says Pedersen, 'is the soul in its outward form.'[1] The body is constitutive of the person and in Hebrew usage it means 'person'. Thus the immortality of the *soul* would denote for a Hebrew that only part of the personality survived death, whereas the resurrection of the body plainly denoted the survival or re-creation of the whole personality. Like content without shape, or music without sound, 'soul' without 'body' would have been meaningless. The Hebrew would have been as baffled by the analytical distinction as Alice was when the Cheshire cat vanished leaving only its smile.

In short, the Bible does not affirm, with Plato, the immortality of the soul since it never thinks of soul and body as separate entities; it does not put asunder what the Creator has joined. 'Body' and 'soul' belong together in their created unity, and neither may be understood apart from the other. That unity is the necessary and perilous workshop of human freedom.

But if the resurrection of the body is a Hebrew concept which sturdily declines to be platonized, what are we to make of it? We must insist that 'body' ($\sigma\tilde{\omega}\mu\alpha$) in this context does not mean what we mean by 'flesh', despite the disastrous *resurrectio carnis* of the Apostles' Creed. The Christian belief in resurrection from the dead cannot mean the restoration in the eternal world of the self-same material elements of which the earthly body is composed, flesh and blood, nerve and brain-cell, this physical framework standing five foot ten and weighing twelve stone. Let me not

---

[1] *Israel* (London, 1926), I, 170.

seem flippant in recalling the charming story of Christina Rossetti's sister, who always refused to visit the mummy room at the British Museum because, as she put it, 'the day of resurrection might suddenly dawn and it would be very unseemly if the corpses had to put on immortality under the gaze of mere sightseers'. What St Paul thought of that mentality seems to be tersely recorded in I Corinthians xv. 35 ff.: 'But someone will ask, How are the dead raised? With what body do they come? Stupid man, what you sow is not the body which is to be. . . . God gives it a body. . . . So it is with the resurrection of the dead; what is sown is perishable; what is raised is imperishable . . . it is sown a physical body; it is raised a spiritual body.'

St Paul's thought, here and elsewhere, is that though death is always the last enemy, even of those who are already 'in Christ' and whose resurrection began long since when they died with Christ at baptism; and though, as God's ordinance for the termination of life's temporal process in this sinful world, death is always inescapable: nevertheless, God will bring the man who is 'in Christ' through this last crisis, giving to him a 'spiritual body', necessarily distinct from its earthly counterpart which perishes, yet somehow inherently continuous with it, and – in a mysterious and ineffable sense – identical with it: much as the wheat-stalk, four feet of golden ripeness from stubble to ear, has continuous, though discontinuous, identity with the bare grain which it was. Resurrection means that the whole self, finally and voluntarily surrendered to God in the sacrifice of death, through Christ's perfect sacrifice, is re-created and reconstituted by God in that order of existence which, as beyond death and time, is beyond all our conceiving; but that in this reconstituted life the whole temporal history of the self is not annulled and lost, but redeemed and fulfilled to the glory of God. St Paul's technical term for the vehicle of this discontinuous continuity is σῶμα. Should it be translated 'body'? Or should we leave it untranslated, and receive its meaning by a familiar analogy (much as St Paul used the analogy of the sown grain)? It has long been known that the actual bodily substance of any living organism is continuously in course of change and renewal. Materially considered, we are not the same even from hour to hour, though the general pattern remains constant. The 'form' is thus continuous although discontinuous; it is independent of 'matter' and yet wholly dependent on it.

Analogy only, and paradoxical at that. Which means that we may receive it only on our knees. For, according to the Hebraic thought of the scriptures, resurrection is miracle. The New Testament points to what is inconceivable by intellect or imagination; the resurrection of Jesus Christ from the dead, in which and to which all those who are in Christ have been conformed and conjoined since their baptism. The Christian religion leaves the Easter mystery as such; and yet it bodies it forth: God, bringing his incarnate Son from the separation of death and hell to his own eternal glory, according to his purpose; and bringing us, the brethren and very Body of Christ, with him. For as in Adam all die, even so in Christ shall all be made alive.

V

Much of the foregoing has had an individual as well as a corporate reference, and this is surely right: it finds its precedent and justification in the New Testament. We may not forget that the man for whom 'the greatest sacrament of all was the Church'[1] was plainly concerned with the resurrection of its individual members in the fifteenth chapter of I Corinthians.

But Dr J. A. T. Robinson's exhaustive analysis of the evidence leaves no doubt that I Corinthians xv does not express the whole mystery and glory of resurrection for St Paul. Its proper individualism is not his only nor his main viewpoint. This classic chapter, to which we rightly give an isolated pre-eminence beside every Christian grave, may seem to support and justify our prejudice that it is our selfhood which has lasting importance. But the main witness of the apostle elsewhere is that just as none of us lives unto himself so 'no man dieth unto himself . . . we are the Lord's'.

[1] R. P. Casey, 'Gnosis, Gnosticism and the New Testament', in *The Background of the New Testament and its Eschatology*, ed. W. D. Davies and D. Daube (Cambridge, 1955), p. 72.

Our resurrection neither begins nor ends with us as individuals. It begins with the Lord and it ends with him, since the ultimate meaning of the resurrection 'body' is the unity of the redeemed universe itself in Christ. The Church on earth and in heaven points to this final unity of all mankind and of all things in him. The goal of the universe is the ending of all estrangement in the *fulness* of reconciliation.

One reason why this ultimate redemption to which the Christian gospel points cannot refer to the individual in isolation, is that it understands and describes redemption as fulfilment. And fulfilment is necessarily universal. It is the final re-establishment or restoration (ἀποκατάστασις) of all that is. What is known, and often bitterly denounced, as Universalism rests on the hardly disputable fact that a *partial* fulfilment of God's redeeming purpose would be a *limited* fulfilment and therefore no fulfilment at all. The concept of partial fulness is not only absurd in logic; it is religiously impossible, for two reasons.

In the first place, it would mean that God's eternal purpose is here defeated. For any soul to persist in its estrangement from God for ever, to reject God's love, and to be finally lost, would mean the failure of the eternal purpose which brought that soul into being. The subtlest dialectic of a Thomas Aquinas or a Jonathan Edwards cannot away with this plain fact. If the parable of the ninety and nine means anything, it means that the eternal loss of one single being would be a limitation of that fulness in Christ which is the goal of all things.

But partial fulfilment seems to be an impossible concept for a second reason. A point which philosophical theology from Origen to Paul Tillich has felt constrained to make is that, limited to selected and separate individuals, fulfilment would not be fulfilment *even for those individuals*, since no single person is separated from other persons in the totality of being. The Catholic Aquinas and the Calvinist Jonathan Edwards are agreed that the saints in glory derive heightened satisfaction from witnessing the punishment of the damned;[1] but, grotesquely horrible and absurd

[1] Edwyn Bevan, *Symbolism and Belief* (Allen and Unwin, 1938), p. 237.

though this is, and typical of all that has made the doctrine of divine judgment abhorrent to the reason and conscience of mankind, the real objection to taking it seriously is that no single person can be saved apart from the salvation of the whole. Even in the eternal order beyond the grave we are still members one of another. To be given a perfect view of the tortures of the damned (*datur eis ut poenas impiorum perfecte videant*, as St Thomas puts it)[1] ignores that point 'at which the destiny of others becomes our own destiny.... And this point is not hard to find. It is the participation of their being in our being. The principle of participation implies that every question concerning individual fulfilment must at the same time be a question concerning universal fulfilment. Neither can be separated from the other'. So Tillich.[2]

The concern of the Christian religion, therefore, is the salvation, not of a few specially gifted individuals, but of the world. The individual is saved only within the kingdom of God, where the risen Christ is τὰ πάντα καὶ ἐν πᾶσι (Col. iii. 11): words which have been translated 'all and in all'; or 'everything and everywhere'; or 'everything for everything'. The Epistle to the Ephesians (i. 23) describes 'the Church which is his Body' as 'filled by him who fills the universe entirely' (τὸ πλήρωμα τοῦ τὰ πάντα ἐν πᾶσι πληρουμένου).

There are Christians who cling earnestly to eternal damnation as a necessary principle and part of Christ's saving gospel; they are dismayed and distressed at any form of the universalist vision that God 'will have all men to be saved'. Even St Paul's statement of double predestination is counterfeit: namely that God hath concluded all in unbelief that he might have mercy upon all. This assumption, that salvation necessarily presupposes damnation for *some*, betrays the legalistic moralism which makes eternal felicity or eternal perdition a matter of desert. Though God's grace in redemption is conceded in principle, eternal blessedness is thought of in fact as something which the redeemed have earned. It is the saints, the faithful remnant within each of the

---

[1] *Summa Theologica*, Supplement to Part III, Qu. 94, Art. i.
[2] *Systematic Theology*, I, 270.

ecclesiastical Confessions, who realize that the Gospel is for sinners, and who understand why Thomas Chalmers once exclaimed, 'What could I do, if God did not "justify the ungodly"?'

Is there no threatening word about the righteousness of the Law, then, in the Gospel of our redemption? Certainly there is. The Gospel never allows us to forget that we come from the Holy One and go to him. We must all stand before the judgment seat of Christ. Men reap what they have sown. God is not mocked. When we have put aside, as unworthy of Christ's gospel of the Kingdom, the Matthaean parable of the sheep and the goats,[1] the New Testament still warns us unambiguously that the consequences of sin can be fearful. Sin is rebellion; and though rebel man goes his way in pride and self-sufficiency to the far country of his alienation, the City of God remains his only real end; and it is not impossible that he should fail to arrive. The Yes of God's Gospel cannot be conceived or stated apart from this No of God's holy Law.

Yet the evangelical logic of God's revelation in Christ is No *and* Yes, rather than Yes *or* No. To the question asked by human logic 'Who then can be saved?' the divine answer is that with God all things are possible. For the final truth, which transcends logic and against which the evil of the world cannot ultimately prevail, is that God is love.

This is perhaps the most difficult, profound and wonderful statement made by our religion. Something of the dialectical tension involved in it comes out in Luther's exegesis of God's 'strange work' in Isaiah xxviii. 21. Through and in his 'strange work' of wrath God does his 'proper work' of love.[2] Luther understands God's holy law in terms of its threefold evangelical function: it is Mirror, Hammer and Mask.

God's love is seen to be wrath and the threat of ultimate destruction to the soul, when the soul sees its rebellious estrangement for what it is, in that Mirror. Only this self-awareness can open

[1] On this see C. H. Dodd, *The Parables of the Kingdom* (Nisbet, 1935), p. 184 and Matthew Arnold's sonnet entitled *The Good Shepherd with the Kid*.

[2] See p. 37 above and *The Protestant Tradition* (Cambridge, 1955), chapter 3, especially pp. 37 – 40.

the door to God's strange work – his wrath of compassion – within the soul. The divine love is against all that is against love; as such it is the Hammer of God's wrath; it leaves the rebel soul to 'destroy' itself; only in this way may the 'destroyed' be saved. For God's wrath is, in the ultimate issue, a Mask; it is the wrath of redeeming love; and in the very acceptance of forgiveness and reconciliation as God's sheer gift, the self-destroying consequences of the soul's refusal of love are overcome. We have to accept God's acceptance of us just as a little child accepts a gift;[1] this is the paradoxical wonder of the gospel of our redemption. God's proper work shines through his strange work; the 'preliminary' act of the Law is, at the same time, the 'ultimate' act of the Gospel.

This means that even in our sinful separation from him God works recreatively, even though this re-creation takes the way of destruction. 'Man', observes Tillich, 'is never cut off from the ground of being; not even in the state of condemnation.'[2] Whether we use the concept of purgatory or not, as we speculate about the mystery of our future being, it is a symbol of the truth we feel after, when we cast ourselves upon the everlasting mercy beyond death

> Where God unmakes, but to remake the soul
> He else made first in vain. . . .[3]

[1] Luke xviii. 17.
[2] *Op. cit.* II, 78.
[3] Robert Browning, *The Ring and the Book: The Pope*, ll. 2131 – 2.

INDEX

Absolutheit des Christentums, 81
Acts of the Apostles, 110 f.
Adam, 98
Addison, 148
'Aergernis der Einmaligkeit', 81
Aeschylus, 22
ἀκίνητον, 2
'Already' *and* 'Not yet', 18
Amos, 84, 91
ἀνάμνησις, 135
animal rationale, 88
animal symbolicum, 88
Ancestors, 108
Anthropology, Greek and Hebrew, 160 f.
Antinomy of Law and Grace, 42–78 *passim*; 34, 37 f., 46
Apocalypse, 12 f.
ἀποκατάστασις, 164
Apostles' Creed, 161
Aquinas, 2, 122, 164 f.
Aristotle, 1, 2, 4, 105
Arnold, Matthew, 5, 142, 166 n.
ἀρραβών, 18
Atomistic conception of man, 110
Atonement, problem of, 75
Aufklärung, 80
Augustine, 1, 6, 10, 20, 39, 82, 133
Aulén, Bishop Gustav, 27

Babel and Pentecost, 113 f.
Babylonian myth of creation, 24 f.
Background of the New Testament and its Eschatology, The (Davies and Daube), 125 n., 128 n., 163 n.
Bainton, R. H., 31
Banquet, the messianic, 135, 145
Baptism, 19, 127–134; as efficacious sign of prevenient grace, 127 ff; of believers, 129, 132
Baptists, 129
Barth, K., 1, 16 f., 129
Bartlet, J. V., 130, 133
Beethoven: The Search for Reality (W. J. Turner), 141
Bérand, 147
Berdyaev, 30
Berengar, 118

Best, E., 157
Bible To-day, The (C. H. Dodd), 89 n., 94 f.
Bigotry, 83
Billerbeck, P., 137
Blake, William, 24, 40
Body, meaning of the, 144
Body of Christ, meaning of the, 144, 148–67 *passim*; 157 f.
Body, The (Robinson), 156 ff.
Bosanquet, B., 6
Bradley, F. H., 20
Brahman, 20
Browning, Robert, 167
Buber, M., 106
Buddhism, 81 f., 85
Bunyan, John, 82, 109
Burke, Edmund, 105

Caiaphas, 64 f.
Caird, G. B., 23, 28 ff., 34
Calvin, 39, 110 f., 121 f., 154
Casey, R. P., 125, 163
Cassirer, E., 88 n.
Catholicism and the sacramental principle, 138
Causality, God's sole, 22, 33
Chalmers, Thomas, 166
China, 85
Chosen People, 85, 90 ff. *See also* Election
Christ: as Cosmic, 95–7; as Criminal, 70; as Curse, 71 f.; as King, 62; as Messiah, 43; as Representative, 59, 145; as Second Adam, 98; as Son of Man, 44;. as Suffering Servant, 67 f., 72, 92; as supreme Sacrament, 125; as Victim, 43 f.; as Victor, 35 f., 71
Christian Year as time-sacrament, 145 f.
Christ in the Universe (Alice Meynell), 96
Church: 98–117 *passim*; 107, 109; as the Body of Christ, 132; as the Brotherhood, 110; as Household of Faith, 132; meaningless if not ultimately universal, 95, 98, 142
Circumcision and Baptism, 131, 133
Clementine Recognitions, 111
Coleridge, 105
Collectivism, 99 ff., 105 f., 107

168

Collingwood, R. G., 6, 106
Community, 105, 108, 111; of the Spirit, 111 f.
Confessions (Augustine), 1
Contemporaneity, 19, 108, 124, 145
Cornford, F. M., 26
Corporate, philosophy of the, 105; in Christian anthropology, 98, 109 f.
Covenant, 8, 48 f.
Creaturely dependence, 140
Cullmann, O., 130 f.

Dalman, G., 137
Damnation, eternal, 165 f.
Daniel, 12 n., 44
Davidson, A. B., 33
Day of Atonement, 50, 53, 74
Dead Sea Scrolls, 5
Death, 27, 73, 148 f.; as natural and unnatural, 149 ff.; as sacrament of time and sacrament of sin, 152; as intrinsically private, 155; the supreme issue of, 151
Demonic, the; 24 ff., 28, 38
Dereliction, the Cry of, 78
'Devotions', 118
Dibelius, M., 27
Didache, The, 139, 142 f.
'Discarnate Intelligences' (Thomas Hardy), 32
Disraeli, 91
Dix, G., 124
Dodd, C. H., 15, 85, 94 f., 136 n., 137, 140, 143, 166 n.
Donne, John, 146
Dragon, The, 25
Dualism, 21 f.

Eastern and Western types of Christianity compared, 79
Economics of capitalist industrialism, 101
Edwards, Jonathan, 164
Eichrodt, W., 50 f.
Einmaligkeit, 80–97 *passim*; 81, 85 f.
Election, biblical meaning of, 91 f.
Encyclopaedists, the, 80
End of history, the, 13 ff.
Eschatology, 12, 18, 21, 23, 117, 135
Essence and Existence, 2 f., 30
'*Est*', the Lutheran, 118
Eucharist, 118–47 *passim*; 19, 118, 120, 134–46; as Commemoration, 122; as Sacrifice, 134; its meaning summarized, 144

Eucharistic theology summarized, 144
Evil, 20 f.; as physical, 149 f.; as moral, 150 f.
Exodus, the, 8, 145
Faith, 128; presupposed in baptism, 128, 131; itself God's gift, 128–9; inherently personal, 132
Forgiveness, 46 f.
Forsyth, P. T., 18, 78
Frazer, J. G., 24 f.
Fricke, O., 140 n.
Fulfilment, 164 f.

Geocentric astronomy, 81
Gerhard, J., 142
Glaucon, 22
Glossolalia, 112 f., 115
God: and Satan, 33 f., 39; as divided against himself?, 22, 38; as *totum simul*, 145
Goethe, 80
Gospel of Redemption, 152 f., 154
Gratia infusa, 121
Greek anthropology, 160 f.
Greek Tragedy (Kitto), 21 f.
Gregory of Nyssa, 39, 41
Ground bass, 134, 136
Guilt, sense of, 105; the guardian of personal identity, 103, 155

ḥăbûrâh, 136
Hebraic anthropology, 161
Hebraism and Hellenism, 2–9, 159
Hebrews, Epistle to the, 56 f.
Hegel, 105
Heim, K., 27 f., 86
Herbert, George, 129
High Priest, 15
History: 1–19 *passim*; 7–9; as nomothetic, 87 f.; as idiographic, 88; as process presupposed by man's rationality, 106
History and the Gospel (Dodd), 146
Höffding, 102
Holy Spirit: *see* Spirit
Hooker, 58
Huxley, T. H., 23

Ideas (Plato), 2
Ideology, bourgeois, 101
Identification of believers with Christ, 50, 127, 138, 154 f.; its twofold meaning, 155 ff., 159

Incarnation, doctrine of the, 58
Individualism, 99 ff., 105, 107, 110, 130
Individuality, human, 102 f.
Infans, 128, 130
Infant baptism, problem of, 128 ff., 132
Inge, Dean, 6, 21, 158
In the End, God . . ., 13 n.
Islam, 81
Israel, the fact of, 90 ff.
Israel (Pedersen), 161 n.

Jeans, Sir James, 88 f.
Jeremias, J., 136 n., 137 f.
Job, 35
Judgment and Renewal, Biblical theme of, 10, 12, 94. *See also* Two-beat rhythm
Justin Martyr, 142 f.

Kant, 30, 82, 100, 105 f.
King-mysticism: in the ancient world, 25; in the Old Testament, 24 f., 27; in the New Testament, 62–7
Kipling, R.; 85
Kittel, G., 81
Kitto, H. D. F., 21
Koestler, A., 91
Köhler, W., 121
Kohlmeyer, 121

Laissez-faire, 101
Lampe, G. W. H., 72, 133
Lavater, 80
Law, 34; of Christ, 116 f.; of the Spirit, 116 f.
Lecerf, A., 10
Leibniz, 100
Leivestad, R., 28
Leviathan: *see* Satan
Liberalism, philosophical and economic, 100 f.
Locke, John, 150 n.
Lost Chord, The, 12
Luke, St, 111 ff.
Luther, 10, 39 ff., 58, 70, 104, 118; his doctrine of the Sacraments, 119 f., 143, 155, 166; his threefold concept of Law, 166 f.

Macbeth, 150
MacMurray, J., 7
Manson, T. W., 136 n.
Marduk, 23 f. *See* Satan

Marx, Karl, 101 f.
Maurice, F. D., 118
Mayor, J. B., 83
Messiah, the, 13 f., 43 f., 62, 108
Metabolism, 143
Metaphors of Redemption (Battlefield, Altar, Law Court), 36 f., 46 f., 69, 78
Meynell, Alice, 96, 141
Micah, 10
Milton, 84
Monism, 20
Monotheism, Hebrew, 22
More, P. E., 6
Moule, C. F. D., 56, 139 n.
Mozley, J. K., 72
Muir, Edwin, 98
Mystery religions, 133
Myth, 32, 38

Nature and Destiny of Man, The (Niebuhr), 150
Nature, as medium of Revelation, 123 f.; meaning of, 144
'Nevertheless', 10 f.
'New': a key-word in the New Testament, 154, 158
New Being, The (Tillich), 17
New Creation, 116
Nicholas II, Pope, 118
Niebuhr, Reinhold, 160
Nietzsche, 31
Noces, Les (Stravinsky), 140
Nota absentis rei and *nota praesentis rei*, 124
Nullum sacramentum sine fide, 121, 128

Obendiek, 27
Ockham's razor, 32
Oman, J., 102
ὁμοούσιος, 142
'Once for all', 86
One Body in Christ (Best), 157
Opus alienum and *opus proprium*, 34, 37, 166
Opus operatum, 52, 133
Oresteia (Aeschylus), 22
Origen, 164
Orphism, 1 f., 8, 55, 159
Otto, R., 90
Outspoken Essays (Inge), 158
Parables of the Kingdom, The (Dodd), 146
Paraclete, 18
Paradox in religion, 18, 34, 36, 38

Participation in Christ's death and resurrection, 59, 137, 145

Particularity of historic Revelation: 80-97 *passim*; the fourfold answer of Christian apologetic to its inherent difficulties, 84 ff., 87 ff.; as structure of our experience, 87 f.; as inexplicably given, 90; as sacrament of universality, 93 ff.

Pascal, 82, 155

Passivity and sacramental action, 127

Passover, 124, 145

Patripassianism, 78

Paul, St, 5, 71 f.

Pedersen, 161

Penal substitution, 70 f.

Penalty, the Cross as, 69 f.

Pentecost, 17, 111 f.

Philip of Macedon, 148

Physics (Aristotle), 1

Pilate, 64 f.

Pilgrim's Progress, The, 109

Piper, O., 31

Plato and Platonism, 1-9, 32, 55, 99, 105, 108 (μέθεξις), 149, 159

Powys, J. C., 31

'Pre-established harmony', 100 f.

Primitive peoples, 140 f.

'Principalities and powers', 26 f., 31 f., 35

Prophets, 8 ff.

Protestantism and the sacramental principle, 138

Puritanism, 9, 148

Pusey, E. B., 118

Quick, O. C., 134

'Radical evil', 30

Raine, Kathleen, 98

Rationalism in the eighteenth century, 80, 82 f.

Realized eschatology, 14 f.

Real Presence, 122, 124, 146

Remembrance (ἀνάμνησις): its ritual significance, 135

Representative, Christ as our, 59, 145

Resurrectio carnis, 161

Resurrection, the, 153 ff.

Resurrection of the Body, 160 ff.

Revelation: through historic actuality, 1, 7-9, 81 f., 85 ff; the problem of its inherent relativity, 82; its claim to uniqueness, 87-97; its offence, 80-89; its supra-historical setting in scripture, 94 f.

Richardson, A., 139

Robinson, J. A. T., 13, 156 f., 158, 163

Robinson, H. W., 161

Sacraments, 118 ff.; as aspects of the theological problem of revelation, 119; as effective signs, 118, 127; as instruments, 124; as outward means of inward grace, 122, 125 f.; their proper and their transcendent meaning, 124 f.; their place in the thought of St Paul, 125; as 'realizing' prevenient grace, 125-8; as 're-presenting' the self-offering of Christ, 134-8; as 'identification' of the believer with the Redeemer's Sacrifice, 138-47; as presupposing human passivity, 127. *See also* Infant baptism, problem of

Sacre du Printemps, Le (Stravinsky), 140

Sacrifice, 42-60; 49; in the prophets, 53 f.; in the Psalter, 54 f., 73; as 'ground bass' of eucharistic theology, 134 f.

Sadler, Sir Michael, 15, 17

Saints in the New Testament, 158

Satan, 18, 24 f., 28 f., 32 f.

Scapegoat, 53

Schamyl, 77

Schopenhauer, 6

Schweitzer, Albert, 27, 157

Schweizer, E., 136 n.

Screwtape, 31

Secondary causes, 22

Self, 99, 105 f., 107; as separate yet participating, 107 f.

'*Significat*', the Zwinglian, 118

Signum, as *philosophicum*, *theologicum* and *efficax*, 124

Simultaneity, 147

Sin, 45 f., 151

Sinai, 8; and Pentecost, 115 ff., 145

'Solidary' *or* 'Societary' conception of man, 105; universal axiom of ancient thought, 130

Son of Man, 44

Sophists, 105

Spencer, Stanley, 147

Spinoza, 6, 20

Spirit, 15-18; the Church as the Community of the, 111 f.; age of the, 116 f.

State, apotheosis of the, 105; natural necessity of, 105

Stauffer, E., 57

Stocks, J. L., 150

INDEX

Stoicism, 4

Stravinsky, 140 f.

Streeter, B. H., 111

Suffering Servant, the, 22, 67 f., 72 f., 74, 92

Suppliants, The (Aeschylus), 22

Swinburne, A. C., 114

Symbolism and Belief (Bevan), 164

Systematic Theology (Tillich), 39 f., 95 f., 165, 167

σῶμα, 161 ff.

Taylor, A. E., 6

Telescoping of time, 10; *see also* Contemporaneity

Temple, the, 8 f., 13, 48

Tertullian, 2, 132

Thought as relatedness, 145

Tillich, P. J., 6, 16, 28, 30, 38 f., 40, 75, 95 f., 138 n., 149, 151 n., 164 f., 167

Time, 1–19 *passim*; 149; and Eternity, 2–8, 19; and Eschatology, 12–19; as a form for the expression of Will, 8–10

Time, Cause and Eternity (Stocks), 150 n.

Togetherness, 105, 107

Torah, The, 145

Totalitarianism, 99, 103 f.

Toynbee, A., 88 f., 95

Trevelyan, G. M., 87

Trinity, Doctrine of the, 57

Troeltsch, E., 81, 88 n.

'Two-beat rhythm', 10, 12, 94

Types of Christianity, Eastern and Western, 79

Universalism, 164 f.

Vaughan, Henry, 123

Verbum, 121

Victoria, Queen, 91

Victorians, 9

Webb, C. C. J., 89

Wesley, John, 109

Western and Eastern types of Christianity contrasted, 79

Word in Reformation theology, the, 119 ff. *See also Verbum*

Wordsworth, William, 5, 141

Wrath of God, 34

Xenophanes of Colophon, 84

Zwingli, 121 f., 134